BATTLES BEFORE GUNPOWDER

JOE KRONE

T0325215

WINGED HUSSAR PUBLISHING, LLC

Cover by V.W.Rospond
Cover Image from the "The Battle of Grunwald" by Juliusz Kossak
Edited by Vincent W. Rospond
Winged Hussar Publishing, LLC, 1525 Hulse Road, Unit 1, Point Pleasant, NJ 08742

This edition published in 2016 Copyright ©Winged Hussar Publishing, LLC

ISBN 978-09903649-2-4
LCN 2015952646
Bibliographical references and index
1.Europe - History, Military. 2. Medieval - History 3. Military - Stategy

TABLE OF CONTENTS

Introduction

When I first discussed the concept of this book with Winged Hussar Publishing I could not help myself and reminisce about the military history books that contained information on memorable battles. These books inspired me because of the fantastic drawings showing hundreds if not thousands of soldiers marching and fighting which in my mind at least accurately portrayed the battles they fought. As a child I imagined recreating these epic conflicts using anything from tiny stones to 1/72 scale toy soldiers. As I got older my passion for military history only grew with age and once I was introduced to miniature wargaming my dreams of playing out the battles came true. I poured over rulebooks trying to determine which game system to use but I found that most compendiums only offered a few historical re-fights and to my chagrin I had no interest in recreating those battles.

The purpose of this book is to give the reader an understanding of why the battles took place, how the battles were fought, and the historical implications of the results. Each battle contains information about the armies that fought and how they were deployed prior to the start of the conflict. In some instances the information for a battle has limited availability but I am hopeful that this presentation will give the reader enough material to successfully organize a great gaming event. The disposition of forces is provided in a 'generic' format so players can take the core composition and apply the data to the game mechanics that they use. Some interpretation was required to format the armies into playable forces for the enjoyment of everyone involved so I encourage all of you to change as many of the details needed to fit the requirements of the gaming group.

The section for recreating the battle is broken down into several components consisting of a ratio, a recommended number of units, the commanders, the forces involved, and the battlefield conditions.

Ratio – The ratio represents an approximation of the forces involved against each other. This ratio can used when adjusting the number of units the players have in mind if they would like to create their own battle.

Number of units – The number of units listed after each of the armies involved is a recommended number of units that would allow for a representative game. The number of units involved could be adjusted up or down using the ratio values to keep the aesthetic of the game intact.

Commanders – These personalities were actively involved commanding hundreds if not thousands of troops during the battle. Some games may only require one commander per army while others need more. Providing the names and which area of the battlefield they controlled gives the players options to determine what they would like to use.

Units – Units can be broken down into infantry, missile infantry, heavy cavalry, light cavalry, and artillery. The terms are purposely left generic because players may want to alter the types of weapons the units possess based on their collections. Infantry represent your melee troops ranging from inexperienced militia to crack men-at-arms. The missile infantry consist of ranged weapons such as bows, longbows, crossbows, slings, and javelins. Heavy cavalry are the hard hitting impact troops that charge at a full gallop into the enemy. They are typically well armed and heavily armored. Light cavalry are lightly armored horsemen or they are wearing no armor at all with each of them equipped with missile weapons, spears, swords, or various hand weapons. The artillery could be trebuchets, bombards, or other rudimentary cannons but for purposes of the recommended units they are not counted as part of the overall unit allowance.

Battlefield Conditions – What often separates one battle from the next are the odd circumstances and random events that impact the outcome of the conflict. Listed under the battlefield conditions is additional information that players may want to incorporate into their game to give the battle a more unique feeling. The concepts are left generic because different rules systems will have different ways of representing the special to work for their rules.

These battles begin at the time of the Fall of Rome in the West, but at the beginning of a very dynamic period of military history. There are several battles within this book that contain the same personalities, but are part of a larger war. Players may wish to link these battles together and create a small campaign having the results of one game impact the setup and disposition of the next. I hope the material provides enough inspiration to offer hours of enjoyment whether you find it interesting to learn more about the wars and their battles, utilize the information to play some fantastic games or inspire you to look more into each action.

Enjoy and all the best,

Joe Krone

Battle of Châlons

AKA: *Battle of Catalaunian Plains (Fields), Battle of Maurica*
Date: *20 June 451*
Where: Champagne-Ardenne region, France

Opponents:
Romans and Visigoths – approximately
50,000 – 80,000 men
Huns – approximately 50,000 – 80,000 men

GAUL 451 A.D.

Background:

The Roman Empire had been in a steady decline for several years and nominally held control of its territory concentrating most of its power along the Mediterranean coastline. The Roman army was no longer legionaries in tight formation, but had begun to copy the weapons, armor and formations of the barbarians they had been fighting. Germanic tribes forced to relocate by stronger adversaries were living on the outskirts of the Roman Empire and serving as foederati to the Emperor. Foederati were given specialized treatment by Rome in exchange for military service which would prove invaluable when the Attila and his Huns attacked.

There are several theories regarding the reason why Attila decided to invade the Roman Empire, but regardless of the motivation his path of destruction was clearly marked. The ancient historian Jordanes believed that the Vandal king Gaiseric convinced Attila to attack the Visigoths while at the same time hoping he would sow discontent between the Visigoths and Western Roman Empire.

Many modern day historians believe that Attila's aggression was motivated in part by pleas from Honoria, the problematic sister of Emperor Valentinian III. She had an arranged marriage with senator Herculanus to keep her confined and under control. She sent word to Attila asking him to free her. In exchange, she would marry Attila and reward him with a dowry of half of the Roman Empire. Attila demanded the release of Honoria along with her promised dowry, but Emperor Valentinian refused. This denial by Valentinian of what Attila perceived as his right to the throne was the only excuse he needed to launch a destructive campaign through Gaul.

Huns attack the Roman line

Early in the year 451 Attila and his army crossed the Rhine and sacked their first city of Divodurum (Metz) on 7 April. Moving through Gaul, Attila reached the fortified city of Aurelianum (Orléans) in June to besiege the city.

Word of this invasion had reached the ears of Magister Militum Flavius Aëtius who gathered his forces and began the march from Italy to Gaul. Along the way Aëtius reached out to friendly barbarian tribes and requested support to help break the siege of Aurelianum. This combined force reached the city of Aurelianum around 14 June just in time to witness Attila's army breaching the city's walls. The Huns had begun to occupy the city but decided to break camp and withdraw in the face of Aëtius' troops. Rome and their barbarian allies followed in close pursuit as Attila looked for an advantageous position to turn and attack.

At the Catalaunian Fields, on 20 June, Attila decided to make his stand and in Hunnic tradition Attila had his diviners examined the entrails of a sacrifice the morning of the battle. It was foretold that the Huns would suffer a great defeat but one of the enemy leaders would die in the battle. Attila's blind hatred for Aëtius and his desire to kill him forced the Huns into battle but not until the sun began to set. Attila hoped that the setting sun would mask his retreat if the Huns were to suffer as the diviners had predicted.

The Catalaunian plain was bound on one side by a steep slope that ended with a ridge. This ridge became the center of the battlefield and early in the battle the Huns seized the right side of the ridge. The Romans occupied the left side of the ridge which left the crest unoccupied by both forces. The Huns advanced along all fronts and made little progress on the right and left flanks but managed to break the center of the Roman army manned by Sangiban and the Alans allied troops.

While leading his Visigoths on the left flank, Theodoric was killed with out his men even noticing and pushed forward to engage Attila's household unit. The strong attack by the Visigoths forced Attila to retreat back to his camp behind his fortified wagons; on the right flank matters were not much better as the Romans under Aëtius pushed past the enemy camp in hot pursuit of the fleeing Huns. As night fell King Theodoric's son Thorismund, accidently mistook the Hun's camp for his own and a small skirmish broke out which resulted in Thorismunnd being wounded before his men could rescue him.

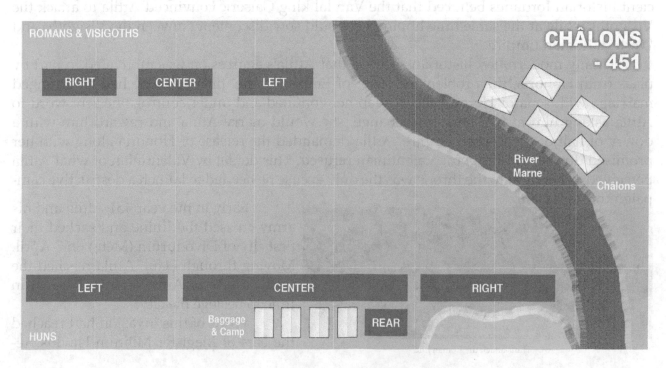

In the morning on the following day, the battlefield was littered with bodies and neither side seemed motivated to attack the other. Attila remained within the fortified camp and prepared a funeral pyre he would use for himself if defeat was imminent as he did not want to give his enemy the satisfaction of taking his life. After Theodoric's body was discovered, Thorismund wanted to immediately renew the attack on the Huns. Instead, Aëtius convinced him to return to Tolosa (Toulouse) with his father's body and claim the throne for himself before his brothers could take action. Aëtius then dismissed his Frankish allies and eventually claimed the battlefield and its treasures for himself. While the battle was inconclusive it has always been portrayed as a great victory which saved Europe because the Romans managed to force the Huns to withdraw from the area.

Wargaming the Battle of Châlons
Ratio – 1:1 (Romans: Huns)

Romans and Visigoths: The Roman army consisted of several barbarian tribes such as the Visigoths, Salian Franks, Ripuarian Franks, Sarmatians, Armoricans, Liticans, Burgundians, Saxons, Librones, and other Celtic and Germanic tribes.

Roman Order of Battle: 20 units

Commanding Officers:
General Flavius Aëtius (Left Flank), Visigothic King Theodoric (Right Flank),Thorismund (Right Flank),Sangiban (Center)

Right Flank	**Left Flank**	**Center**
8 units of infantry	7 units of infantry	3 units of infantry
1 unit of light cavalry	1 unit of light cavalry	

Late Roman infantry defend a hill

Huns: The Huns, similarly to the Roman army consisted of several tribes such as Rugians, Gepids, Gelonians, Burgundians, Sciri, Bellonotians, Neurians, Bastarnae, Thuringians, Bructeri, and Franks.

Hun Order of Battle: 20 units

Commanding Officers:
Attila (Center), Walamir, Theodemir, and Widimir (Left Flank), Ardaric (Right Flank)

Right Flank	**Left Flank**	**Center**
4 units of infantry	5 units of infantry	6 units of light cavalry
2 units of light cavalry	1 unit of light cavalry	

Rear
Attila's fortified wagon camp with 2 units of infantry

Battlefield Conditions

Setting Sun – The battle did not commence until the sun was beginning to set so players could incorporate night time conditions making visibility and archery distances much shorter.

Friend or Foe – Once darkness falls on the battlefield the soldiers can become easily confused on their location and if the units around them are friend or foe. Players may want to include special conditions forcing units to take a morale or leadership test before they can successfully charge or shoot at the enemy.

Hun cavalry charges the Roman battle line

Flanking Force – Thorismund and his retinue got turned around during the battle after the sunset and accidently mistook Attila's camp for his own. If players are using the Setting Sun condition then Thorismund and his units are held off table in reserve to come into play after the battle has started. If players are not using the Setting Sun condition then Thorismund and his two units will fall under the command of King Theodoric.

Heir to the Throne – If Theodoric is killed during the battle it becomes very important for Thorismund to return home as quickly as possible to claim the throne before his brothers can react to the loss of their father and king. Players may want to force a leadership or morale test each turn in order for Thorismund to remain on the battlefield or if Theodoric is killed Thorismund and his units will be removed from the game.

The Commanders

Flavius Aëtius was born at Durostorum in Moesia Inferior (modern Silistra, Bulgaria), around 391. His father, was a Roman general of Gothic origin. Prior to 449 Aetius allowed some Huns to settle in Pannonia, along the Sava River and corresponded with Attila. Aetius persuaded the Visigoths and several other Germanic tribes to thwart the Hun's thrust into Gaul in 451. In 452 Attila attacked through the Julian Alps to invade Italy. Although he still commanded Rome's forces he was not able to bring the Huns to another decisive battle and it was only through the negotiations with Pope Leo (along with disease) that forced the Huns to retreat. He was murdered by or on the orders of Valentinian III in 454, who believed Aetius was trying to usurp him.

Attila was the ruler of the Hunnic Empire that stretched from the Ural to Rhine Rivers, reigning from 434 until his death in March 453. Starting in the late 430's he attacked the Eastern Roman Empire and Persia before invading the Western Empire, which culminated in his defeat at the Catalaunian Plains in 451 After failing to take Rome in 452 he retreated north, but died before he could renew the attack in 453. The Hunnic Empire quickly collapsed after his death.

Flavius Aetius

Atilla, "The Scourge of God"

Battle of Tours

AKA: *Battle of Poitiers*
Date: 10 October 732
Where: Between Tours and Poitiers, France

Opponents:
Franks – approximately 30,000 men
Umayyad Caliphate – approximately 55,000 men

Background:

KINGDOM OF
FRANKS 732 A.D.

From 711-718, Tariq ibn-Ziyad, leader of the Umayyads, sailed across the Strait of Gibraltar and began the expansion of the Muslim influence over the Visigothic Kingdom of Hispania. For the next 21 years the Umayyad caliphate was busy conquering parts of Europe including the Iberian Peninsula. The Arabs moved northward into Aquitaine and Burgundy, but suffered a setback when Duke Odo of Aquitaine broke their siege at Toulouse. The Umayyad quickly resupplied their forces and by 725 they advanced as far as Autun in Burgundy. Duke Odo was fighting a two-front war with the Umayyads in the south and the Franks in the north so he decided to ally himself with the Berber emir Uthman ibn Naissa. Unfortunately, Uthman rebelled against the governor of al-Andalus, 'Abd-el-Rahmân, and was quickly crushed allowing Rahmân to concentrate his efforts against Acquitaine. Duke Odo assembled his army to defend his lands, but he was defeated at Bordeaux resulting in the city being plundered. Odo turned to the Franks and not only warned Charles Martel of the impending invasion but asked for his assistance in repulsing the Muslims. Martel agreed to help, but the Muslims were unaware of the Franks true strength and unfamiliar with their fighting prowess until they met them on the field of battle at Poitiers.

The Umayyad began by marching towards the Loire River at which point several raiding parties splitting off from the slower moving main army. The Muslims devastated southern Gaul including the sack of the Abbey of Saint Martin of Tours, one of the most prestigious

Frank cavalry attacking the Muslim invaders

and holiest shrines in Western Europe. Charles Martel amassed his troops and marched south avoiding the main roads in order to surprise the Muslims and select the battlefield that complimented his fighting style.

The Umayyad army moved to attack Tours, but along their way they were surprised by a large Frankish force that was well deployed, prepared for battle, on high ground, and directly opposing their advance. The Franks were arranged in a phalanx-like formation with hills and trees to their front to break up the charges of the Muslim cavalry. The two armies squared off against each other for seven days with only minor skirmishes occurring because'Abd-al-Rahmân was hesitant to attack such a well prepared enemy and he was waiting for the rest of his army to arrive. Rahmân recalled all of his troops until he could ascertain the true strength of the Frankish army but this delay allowed Charles time to receive his veteran infantry from the distant areas of his kingdom.

The Frankish line in the attack

Neither commander wanted to press the attack but Rahmân's desire to sack Tours outweighed Martel's desire to leave his defensive position. Charles had been preparing for this situation since the Battle of Toulouse ten years earlier and his veteran infantry were critical to his success. The Franks had no heavy cavalry and Martel's militia was useless against a cavalry charge. Charles has been training his army for a decade and they were very familiar with the Muslims fighting capabilities, but Rahmân knew almost nothing about the Franks.

Rahmân decided to attack on the seventh day of both armies facing each other because delaying any longer would risk his army falling prey to the winter conditions. He trusted the fact that his cavalry had performed admirably in previous battles so Rahmân relied on them to wear down the Franks through repeated charges with their long lances and swords. The Muslim cavalry repeatedly crashed into the Frank infantry formations and each time they were repulsed. The year-round training of the Franks received played a huge role in their successful defense because up till then no other enemy was able to withstand the charge of Umayyad heavy cavalry.

At the height of the battle a rumor spread through the Umayyad army that Frankish scouts had penetrated the Muslim lines and threatened to capture the booty that was taken

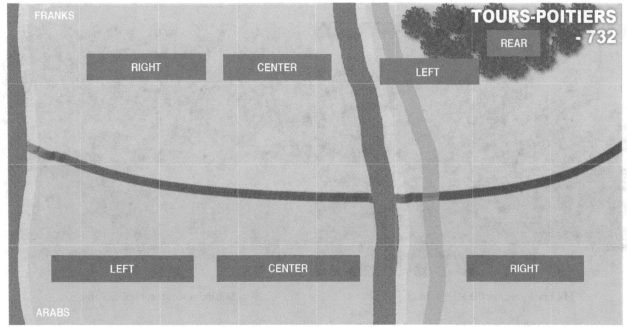

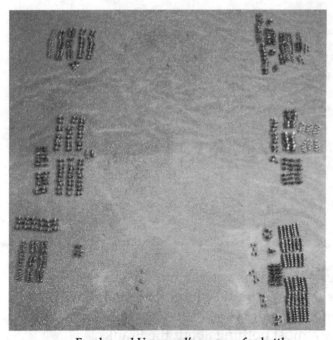

Franks and Umayyad's prepare for battle

from Bordeaux. Several units of Umayyad troops broke off from combat and returned to camp to secure the loot. Under this cover, Charles sent raiding parties to free as many of the captured slaves as possible with the hopes of drawing off Muslim cavalry from the main combat. This plan worked perfectly as many of the Umayyad cavalry viewed the withdrawal as a full scale retreat which in turn became a rout. Rahmân attempted to halt the retreat but ended up surrounded byFrankish soldiers and was cut down during the chaos. The Muslims returned to their camp on the following day, but Charles resisted the temptation to move his forces down the hill to engage the enemy. After an extensive reconnaissance of the area the Frankish soldiers only found a hastily abandoned camp as the Umayyad army slipped away, marching back to Iberia with what treasure remained.

Charles Martel and the Franks continued to press the advantage and they launched two more campaigns in 736 and 739 re-conquering most of the territories lost to the Muslims except for the city of Narbonne. For the next twenty-seven years the Umayyad held Narbonne until it finally fell to Charles' son, Pippin the Short, in 759. In 768, Pippin died leaving his son Charlemagne the king of the Franks to usher in a new era of Christendom to Europe.

The Franks engage the Muslim lines

Muslim forces receive the charge

Wargaming the Battle of Tours
Ratio – 3:5 (Franks:Arabs)

Franks Order of Battle: 12 units

Commanding Officers:
Charles Martel; Odo, Duke of Aquitaine

Right Flank	Left Flank	Center	Rear
3 units of infantry	3 units of infantry	4 units of infantry	2 units of light cavalry

Arab Order of Battle: 20 units

Commanding Officers:
Abd Al-Rahmân Ghafiqi

Right Flank:	LeftFlank:	Center:
2 units of heavy cavalry	2 units of heavy cavalry	6 units of light cavalry
2 units of light cavalry	2 units of light cavalry	2 units of infantry
2 units of infantry	2 units of infantry	

Battlefield Conditions

Wooded and Uphill: Charles Martel had been training his army for years in preparation for a showdown against the Umayyad. He maneuvered his army to select the best ground for his troops. The Arabs were forced to attack uphill and through a field that was spotted with trees hindering a truly effective cavalry charge. Players may wish to incorporate a movement penalty for the Arabs when moving or charging uphill.

Treasure Horde: The Arabs were concerned about losing their recently acquired treasure for sacking Bordeaux and to reflect their motivation players may want to place a turn limit on the game. If the Arabs cannot secure victory by a particular turn then word spreads that their baggage train is being sacked and Arab units must leave the battlefield to secure their treasure. Units would be required to take a morale or leadership test to remain in the game once the assigned turn has been reached.

The Commanders

Charles Martel (c. 688 or 686, 680 – 22 October 741) was a Frankish statesman and military leader who, as Duke and Prince of the Franks and Mayor of the Palace, was de facto ruler of Francia from 718 until his death in 741. He was born in Herstal between 680 and 688 as the son of a Frankish official. Although Charles never assumed the title of king, he divided Francia, like a king, between his sons Carloman and Pepin. The latter became the first of the Carolingians, the family of Charles Martel, to become king.

Charles helped to unify Gaul and then turned to Arab incursions to the south. After Tours, Charles took to the offensive, destroying fortresses at Agde, Béziers and Maguelonne, although he failed to recover Narbonne (737). He is considered a skilled administrator as well as a warrior; credited with key role in the development of the feudal system.

Abdul Rahman Al Ghafiqi, also known as Abd er Rahman, Abdderrahman, Abderame, and Abd el-Rahman, unsuccessfully led the Andalusian Muslims into battle against the forces of Charles Martel in the Battle of Tours on October 10, 732 AD. Arab historians praise Abdul Rahman as a just and able administrator and commander. Without his leadership and guidance, the other commanders were unable even to agree on a commander to lead them back into battle the morning after the battle at Tours. His son attempted another invasion of Gaul under the Caliph's instructions in 736, this time by sea.

Charles Martel

Abdul Rahman Al Ghafiqi

Battle of Brunanburh

Date: October 937
Where: Between Bromborough and Bebington in Merseyside, England

Opponents:

Kingdom of England (Anglo-Saxon) – approximately 15,000 men

Kingdoms of Dublin, Alba, and Strathclyde (Celts–Norse) – approximately 15,000 men

Background:

Æthelstan of England had defeated the Vikings at York in 927 and King Constantine of Scotland, King Hywel Dda of Deheubarth, Ealdred of Bamburg, and King Owain of Strathclyde accepted Æthelstan's lordship as King of the English. A period of relative peace lasted until 934 when Æthelstan invaded Scotland because King Constantine broke the treaty accepting him as overlord. The invasion prompted the King of Dublin, Olaf Guthfrithsson, Scottish King Constantine II, and Owen of Strathclyde to ally themselves against Æthelstan to quell the threat.

After Olaf Guthfrithsson defeated the Norse king Amlaib Cenncairech at Limerick in August of 937 he sailed his army to join with the forces of Constantine and Owen. The armies of Constantine and Owen marched toward England following the Roman road across the Lancashire plains meeting Olaf along the way.

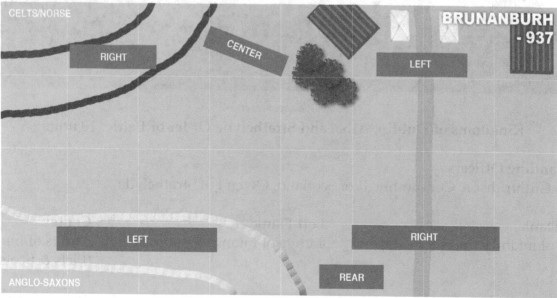

There is little information available detailing the accounts of the battle but it is known as one of the bloodiest battles to be fought on British soil. Even the location of the battle site is under debate but what is known is that the Celtic/Norse forces of Olaf, Constantine, and Owen fortified their encampment with timber reinforced trenches. These positions were quickly overrun by Æthelstan's forces and the momentum of the attack sealed victory for the Anglo-Saxons. The Battle of Brunanburh is believed to be the first time that a British Army deployed cavalry in battle but this topic is highly speculative. In the end, five kings and seven earls laid dead on the battlefield with both armies suffering devastating losses. Æthelstan's victory at the Battle of Brunanburh legitimized England as a unified kingdom but the vast amount of casualties weakened his ability to maintain control over the British Isles. Æthelstan consolidated his reign resulting in the countries of England, Scotland and Wales exist today.

Wargaming the Battle of Brunanburh
Ratio – 1:1 (Anglo-Saxons:Celts/Norse)

Kingdom of England Order of Battle: 10 units

Commanding Officers:
Æthelstan of England, Edmund I of England

Right Flank
5 units of infantry (West Saxons)

Left Flank
4 units of infantry (Shire Levies)

Rear
1 unit of cavalry

Battle lines are set

Kingdoms of Dublin, Alba, and Strathclyde Order of Battle: 10 units

Commanding Officers:
Olaf III Guthfrithson, Constantine II of Scotland, Owen I of Strathclyde

Right Flank
3 units of infantry (Picts & Scots)

Left Flank
4 units of infantry (Vikings)

Center
3 units of infantry (Picts & Scots)

Battlefield Conditions

Trenches: The Celts and Norse fortified their position by digging trenches and reinforcing them with timbers. The defenses had little significance over the result of battle but players may wish to incorporate them to see if they can create a different historical outcome.

Battles lines are in position as champions fight to open the battle

The Commanders

Æthelstan or *Athelstan* (c. 894 – 27 October 939) was King of the Anglo-Saxons from 924 to 927 and King of the English from 927 to 939. He was the grandson of Alfred the Great. Many historians regard him as the first King of England and one of the greatest Anglo-Saxon kings. He never married, and was succeeded by his half-brother, Edmund. Although Æthelstan's seems to have been revered during his lifetime, his reign was quickly pushed to the background and lumped into that of several underwhelming successors.

Athelstan

Olaf Guthfrithsson was a member of the Norse-Gael Uí Ímair dynasty and King of Dublin from 934 to 941. He succeeded his father, Gofraid ua Ímair, as King of York in 927 following the death of his kinsman Sitric Cáech, but was expelled in the same year by King Æthelstan of England. In August 937 Olaf defeated his Norse rivals based at Limerick, and became allied with King Constantine II of Scotland through marriage, as well as Owen I of Strathclyde. In the autumn 937, Olaf led his allies into battle against Æthelstan in the Battle of Brunanburh and was decisively defeated.

After Athelstan's death in 939, Olaf invaded York again, forcing Athelstan's successor, Edmund, into a treaty which ceded Northumbria and part of Mercia to Olaf. He died two years later in 941, succeeded by Amlaíb Cuarán. There has been speculation that a skeleton found at Auldhame, East Lothian in Scotland may be that of Guthfrithsson.

Battle of Lechfeld

AKA: *Second Battle Of Augsburg*
Date: 10 August 955
Where: Augsburg, Bavaria, Germany

Opponents:
East Francia and Bohemia –
        approximately 8,000 men
Magyars –   approximately 17,000 men

Background:

In the 890's the Turkic Magyar tribes migrated into Carpathia and for the next 50 years they tormented the Saxons and Bavarians launching raids into their lands when needed supplies. By the early 950s Henry I and his son Otto had launched campaigns to push back the Magyars and unify the Germanic duchies into what would become the Eastern Frank Kingdom.

In 954 Otto was confronted with a new problem because Duke Conrad of the Franks raised a rebellion and allied himself with the Magyars. Conrad later repented for his rebellion but the Magyars were unleashed and needed to be stopped. Otto's Saxon troops were already engaged down on the Slavic frontier so he quickly pieced together a small army of Bavarians, Franks, Swabians, Bohemians, and his own personal Saxon household to intercept the Magyars.

Otto raised approximately an 8,000 man force broken up into eight 1,000-strong divisions (legiones) consisting of three from Bavaria lead by Henry I, Duke of Bavaria; two from Swabia under the command of Burchard III, Duke of Swabia; one from Franconia, and one from Bohemia under the generalship of Prince Boleslav I. The eighth division was led by Otto and was slightly larger than the others consisting of Saxons, Thuringians, Otto's personal guard and a contingent of Frankish knights commanded by Duke Conrad.

The Hungarian Magyar army was a larger force of perhaps between 10-25,000 men. They moved up the Iller River and began to siege Augsburg which was defended by Bishop Ulrich. On 8 August at the eastern gate of the city a fierce battle broke out with a large number of Hungarians attempting to storm Augsburg. The Germans successfully defended the city after they killed the Hungarian leader and forced them to withdraw. The following day the Hungarians attacked the city from all different angles, but their assault was suspended when Berchtold of Risinesburg arrived with the vanguard of the German army.

Ottonian Battle line

The Germans marched into battle with the three divisions of Bavarians in the front followed by the Franks, Saxons, Swabians, and Bohemians. The divisions were deployed in a single line with no reserves while the Bohemians were responsible for defending the camp and baggage. The mounted Hungarians moved forward in a traditional horse archer formation firing arrows into the German knights. The frontal attack was merely a distraction because the main attack was a flanking force sent to the rear of the German army. The Magyars sent a portion of their force across the Lech River to the rear of the German column and initially attacked the Bohemians routing Bolesalv's knights. The Hungarians flank attack advanced into the Swabians from the rear while the remaining Magyars attacked the front of the German column. The Swabians became disorganized but remained in control and fell back towards Otto's own division. When Otto received word that the Hungarians attacked the rear of the army, he ordered Conrad to conduct a flanking maneuver to aid the Swabians and regain control of the baggage train before returning to the main force. The pincer move conducted by Conrad and the Swabians cutoff the Hungarians and they were subsequently destroyed.

Otto did not hesitate launching a frontal assault and pushing through a volley of arrows the Germans charged into the Hungarian line catching them off guard. Having disposed of the Hungarian flanking force Conrad returned to the front and lead a charge with his knights before being brought down by an arrow in the throat. The Magyars were unprepared for the Germans determined hand-to-hand fighting as they were unable to employ their traditional shoot-and-run tactics. One of the Hungarian leaders named, Bulcsú attempted to goad the Germans into breaking their line by feigning a retreat but the Germans maintained order and continued to push the Magyars from the field. The Germans kept up the pressure over the next few days and continued to pursue the Hungarians in a well-disciplined mass. Otto ordered that all the river crossings should be guarded so that as many of the Hungarians as possible could be captured and killed before they escaped back to Hungary. When the Magyars were captured they were either executed or sent back mutilated to their ruling prince, Taksony, who recently took the crown after the former Hungarian leader Fajsz was overthrown. The Hungarian dukes Lél, Bulcsú, and Sur were not from the ruling Árpáds dynasty so they were executed because of their lack of political influence.

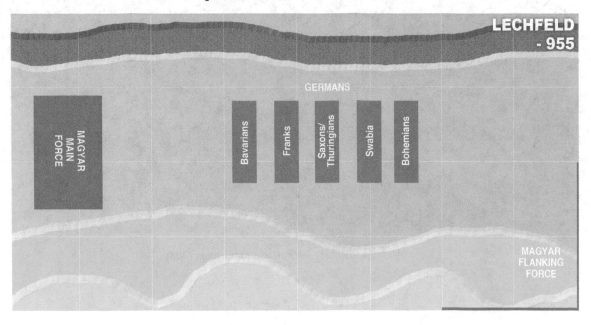

After the battle Otto was lifted upon the shields of the nobles and declared emperor but it took a few more years before Otto traveled to Rome and was crowned Holy Roman Emperor by Pope John XII. Otto never endeavored to launch a campaign against Hungary and the loss at Lechfeld ended nearly a 100 year long Hungarian military dominance in Europe. The battle's outcome played a pivotal role in holding off the Hungarian invasions into Western Europe and introduced a new style of combat with knightly cavalry becoming the key component in the future of warfare.

Wargaming the Battle of Lechfeld
Ratio – 1:2 (Germans: Magyars)

German Order of Battle: 9 units

Commanding Officers:
Otto I the Great (Saxons & Thuringians), Henry I, Duke of Bavaria (Bavarians),Burchard III, Duke of Swabia (Swabia), Prince Boleslav I (Bohemians), Duke Conrad the Red (Franks)

March Column Order
3 units of infantry (Bavarians) 1 unit of heavy cavalry (Franks)
2 units of infantry (Saxons, Thuringians, Otto's bodyguard) 2 units of infantry (Swabia)
1 unit of infantry and baggage train (Bohemians)

A Magyar flanking force attacks the German lines

Magyar Order of Battle: 18 units

Commanding Officer:
Duke Bulcsú, Duke Lél, Duke Súr

Main Force
4 units of infantry
6 units of light cavalry
2 units of heavy cavalry

Flanking Force
4 units of light cavalry
2 units of heavy cavalry

Battlefield Conditions

Narrow Frontage: The Germans were aware that they were outnumbered and they marched by division in single file through a narrow pass over rough ground to reduce the effectiveness of the Magyars cavalry charges. Players may want to consider playing the game along a narrow frontage to simulate the tactics used during the battle.

Flank Attack: The Magyars attacked the head of the German column with the intent of pinning them in place so their flanking force could whip around to the rear and deal a crushing blow. The Magyar player may wish to hold the Flanking Force in reserve and bring on the units using the appropriate rules.

A 15th century German depiction of Lechfeld

Otto in the field commanding his forces

The Commanders

Otto I (23 November 912 – 7 May 973), also known as Otto the Great, was German king from 936 and emperor of the Holy Roman Empire from 962 until his death in 973. Otto was "the first of the Germans to be called the emperor of Italy". Otto inherited the Duchy of Saxony and the kingship of the Germans upon his father's death in 936 and continued his father's work of unifying all German tribes into a single kingdom; greatly expanded the king's powers at the expense of the aristocracy. Through strategic marriages and personal appointments, Otto installed members of his family in the kingdom's most important duchies.

After putting down a brief civil war among the rebellious duchies, Otto defeated the Magyars at the Battle of Lechfeld in 955, thus ending the Hungarian invasions of Western Europe. The victory against the pagan Magyars earned Otto a reputation as a savior of Christendom and secured his hold over the kingdom. By 961, Otto had conquered the Kingdom of Italy and extended his realm's borders to the north, east, and south. The patronage of Otto and his immediate successors facilitated a limited cultural renaissance of the arts and architecture. Following the example of Charlemagne's coronation as "Emperor of the Romans" in 800, Otto was crowned Emperor in 962 by Pope John XII in Rome.

Bulcsú (or *Vérbulcsú*; died 10 August 955) was a Hungarian chieftain and military leader of medieval Hungary who was also a descendant of Árpád. He was a key figure the Magyar invasions of the tenth century, but was executed after the disastrous Battle of Lechfeld.

Otto I

Bulcsú

Battle of Hastings

Date: 14 October 1066
Where: Hastings, East Sussex, England

Opponents:
Normans – approximately 7,000 -12,000 men
English – approximately 5,000 – 13,000 men

Background:

Norman foreign policy was very interested in English politics since 1002 when King Æthelred II of England married Emma, the sister of Richard II, Duke of Normandy. Their son Edward spent several years in exile in Normandy but when he succeeded to the English throne in 1042 he placed several Normans into influential roles. Edward had his enemies and the increase of Norman influence created even more tension forcing him into a conflict with the great Saxon families such as Godwin, Earl of Wessex, and his sons.

The death of King Edward the Confessor on 5 January 1066 left the English throne vacant and without an heir apparent but Edward's Queen Edith's brother and the son of Godwin, Harold Godwinson was elected king shortly after Edward's death. His reign was immediately threatened by William II of Normandy, his own brother Tostig, and the Norwegian King Harald Hardrada (Harold III of Norway). Hardrada and Tostig moved against the English earning a quick victory at the Battle of Fulford on 20 September 1066 against the English commanders Edwin and Morcar.

Shieldwalls meet

Harold was anticipating an invasion by William and was originally camped with an army on the southern coast of England in early September when he released the majority of his militia because they needed to go home and harvest their crops. Once he received word that Tostig and the Norwegians were invading; Harold hastily moved north gathering troops along his route. On 25 September at the Battle of Stamford Bridge, King Harold destroyed the alliance of Tostig and Harald Hardrada and took their lives leaving William as the only serious contender. While Harold's army was recuperating from the battle, William, who felt entitled to the English crown, realized his opportunity to invade and on 28 September he landed an army at Pevensey prepared to conquer England.

Skirmishers advance on the Saxon position

Harold left the majority of his army with Edwin and Morcar in the north of England while he moved south quickly to intercept William. During the two weeks it took him to travel to the southern coast he assembled a new army and positioned himself at the top of Senlac Hill approximately six miles from the castle that William built at Hastings. Half of William's army consisted of infantry spearmen and a quarter each of cavalry and archers. It marched from Hastings to meet the English force comprised of mostly infantry and some archers. At 9 am on Saturday, 14 October, 1066 the armies met one another with Harold's forces deployed in a dense linear formation forming a shield wall on the top of Caldbec Hill with their flanks protected by woods and a stream with a marsh lying to their front. The English axemen interlocked their shields with archers and men with javelins standing behind the protection of the wall waiting for the Normans to advance.

The Normans formed into three 'battles' essentially based on the origins of the troops. The left flank consisted of men from Breton, Anjou, Poitou, and Maine led by the Breton count, Alan the Red. The center of the army was controlled by William and his soldiers from Normandy while the men from France, Picardy, Boulogne, and Flanders deployed on the right flank under the generalship of William fitz Osbem and Count Eustace II of Boulogne.

The Norman army advanced with their archers, crossbowmen, and slingers in the front supported by spearmen and the cavalry held in reserve. They opened the battle with a volley

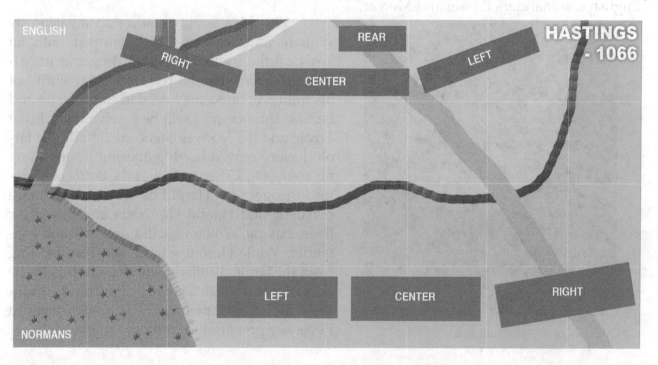

of archery fire but it had little effect on the English because of their shield wall and the difficulty of shooting uphill. Next, William sent the spearmen in and they were met by a barrage of thrown spears, axes, and stones. The two sides collided and the Norman spearmen were unable to create any openings for the cavalry to exploit but with the line faltering William charged his cavalry with the hope of tipping the balance of the conflict in his favor. The combined arms attack of the Norman army failed to push the English back and a rumor had spread that William had been killed causing confusion among the ranks. The Normans began a general retreat with the English in pursuit until William rode through his army rallying his forces and ordering a counter-attack.

By midday both forces were exhausted, needing time to rest and take on some food and water. The break gave both Harold and William time to contemplate a new strategy before the battle recommenced. The Norman army implemented a tactic that they have used successfully

Charge of Breton cavalry

Norman forces move forward

in the past consisting of a cavalry charge followed by a retreat hoping to draw the English shieldwall out of position. These feigned attacks were conducted several times but they could not break the English line until late in the afternoon when Harold was killed and the English army began to collapse. The Normans pursued the fleeing Englishmen, but the royal household (Huscarls) held fast and defended Harold's body until the bitter end. The rout of the English army ended the Battle of Hastings but it took several more battles before William was crowned King of England on 25 December 1066 in Westminster Abbey. His troubles did not end at Hastings because over the next four years William was forced to put down rebellions that challenged his right to rule over England.

A section of the Bayeux Tapestry showing Saxon infantry holding off William's cavalry

Wargaming the Battle of Hastings
Ratio – 1:1 (Normans: English)

Norman Order of Battle: 12 units

Commanding Officers:

William of Normandy (Center), Alan the Red, Count of Breton (Left Flank),William fitz Osbem & Eustace II, Count of Boulogne (Right Flank)

Right Flank (French & Flemish)	Left Flank (Bretons)	Center (Normans)
2 units of infantry	2 units of infantry	2 units of infantry
1 unit of missile infantry	1 unit of missile infantry	
2 units of heavy cavalry	2 units of heavy cavalry	

English Order of Battle: 12 units

Commander Officers:

Harold Godwinson (Center), Gyrth Godwinson (Right Flank), Leofwine Godwinson (Left Flank)

Right Flank	Left Flank	Center	Rear
2 units of infantry	2 units of infantry	2 units of infantry	2 units of heavy cavalry
2 units of missile infantry	2 units of missile infantry		

Battlefield Conditions

None. The armies were evenly matched and other than the Normans attacking up hill there were no outside influences that affected the outcome of the battle.

Norman cavalry charging

The Commanders

Harold II (or *Harold Godwinson*; 1022 – 14 October 1066) was the last Anglo-Saxon king of England. Harold reigned from 6 January 1066 until his death at the Battle of Hastings on 14 October. Harold was a powerful earl and member of a prominent Anglo-Saxon family with ties to King Cnut. Upon the death of Edward the Confessor in January 1066, the Witenagemot convened and chose Harold to succeed; he was crowned in Westminster Abbey. In late September he successfully repelled an invasion by rival claimant Harald Hardrada of Norway, before marching his army back south to meet William the Conqueror at Hastings some two weeks later.

William I (c. 1028 – 9 September 1087), also known as *William the Conqueror* and sometimes *William the Bastard*, was the first Norman King of England, reigning from 1066 until his death in 1087. The descendant of Viking raiders, he had been Duke of Normandy since 1035. After a long struggle to establish his power, by 1060 his hold on Normandy was secure, and he launched the Norman conquest of England in 1066. The rest of his life was marked by struggles to consolidate his hold over England and his continental lands and by difficulties with his eldest son.

After further military efforts William was crowned king on Christmas Day 1066, in London. He made arrangements for the governance of England in early 1067 before returning to Normandy. He did not try to combine his lands as one domain, but administered each separately. Several unsuccessful rebellions followed, but by 1075 William's hold on England was mostly secure, allowing him to spend the majority of the rest of his reign on the continent. After his death, William's lands were divided amongst his sons: Normandy went to his eldest, Robert, and his second surviving son, William, received England.

Harold II

William I

Battle of Las Navas deTolosa

Date: 16 July 1212
Where: Las Navas de Tolosa, Jaén, Andalusia

Opponents:
Christians – approximately 12,000 – 14,000 men
Moors – approximately 22,000 – 30,000 men

Background:

During the 12th century a Muslim expansion called the Almohad movement started in Morocco and spread into the Iberian Peninsula. By 1195, Alfonso VIII of Castile was defeated by the Almohads at the Battle of Alarcos and soon after the Muslims took the key cities Trujillo, Plasencia, Talavera, Cuenca and Uclés. In 1211, Muhammad al-Nasir amassed a powerful Muslim army in Morocco and crossed the Strait of Gibraltar invading Christian territory and capturing the Calatrava Knights stronghold in Salvatierra. The progress of the Almohads alarmed Pope Innocent III and the threat became real enough for the pontiff to call a crusade of European knights to defend the Christian kingdoms on the Iberian Peninsula.

Under the leadership of Alfonso VIII the crusaders marched through the Despeña Perros Pass, which was shown to them by a local shepherd and pounced on the unsuspecting Moorish camp. The Muslim army was taken by complete surprise and to stave off the attackers the Caliph Muhammad al-Nasir had his tent surrounded by a bodyguard of slave-warriors who were chained together as defense. King Sancho VII led a force of Navarrese Christians who broke through the lines and crushed the Caliph's defenders. Muhammad al-Nasir escaped the carnage and eventually made his way back to Morocco where he ended up dying in Marrakesh.

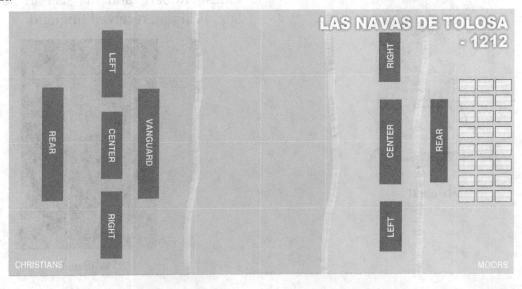

The Moors were dealt a serious blow at the Battle of Las Navas de Tolosa with thousands of dead Muslims strewn across the battlefield. The Christians suffered far fewer casualties with the Knightly Orders suffering the worst. These horrendous losses excellerated the decline of the Almohad Empire and in the years to come the Christians retook major fortified cities such as Baeza and Úbeda in Iberia. Alfonso VIII's grandson, Ferdinand III of Castile, picked up the campaign and liberated Cordova in 1236, Jaén in 1246, and Seville in 1248. Ferdinand's successes encouraged him to sail across the Strait of Gibraltor and bring the war to the heart of the Almohad Empire but his premature death ended the invasion plans. By 1252 the Almohad Empire had lost all of its influence and a new power, the Marinid, was emerging in Africa. They attempted to reclaim the territory that the former Almohad Empire owned on the Iberian Peninsula but Alfonso XI of Castille and King Afonso IV of Portugal crushed their attempt at the Battle of Rio Salado in1340.

Wargaming the Battle of Las Navas deTolosa
Ratio- 1:2 (Christians: Moors)

Christian Order of Battle: 12 units

Commanding Officer:
Alfonso VIII of Castile (Rear), Nuñez de Lara (Center), Diego López de Haro (Vanguard) Sancho VII of Navarre (Right Flank), Pedro II of Aragón (Left Flank)

Right Flank (Navarrese)
1 unit of infantry
1 unit of heavy cavalry

Left Flank (Aragonese)
1 unit of infantry
1 unit of light cavalry

Center (Military Orders)
1 unit of infantry
1 unit of heavy cavalry

Rear (Castilian)
2 units of heavy cavalry

Vanguard
1 unit of infantry
3 units of heavy cavalry

Christian forces form a battleline

Moor Order of Battle: 24

Commanding Officer:
Muhammadal-Nasir

Right Flank
4 units of light cavalry (Turkish archers, Almohad)
1 unit of infantry (Andalusis/foreign volunteers)
1 unit of missile infantry (Berber light infantry)

Left Flank
4 units of light cavalry (Turkish archers, Almohad)
1 unit of infantry (Andalusis/foreign volunteers)
1 unit of missile infantry (Berber lightinfantry)

Center
2 units of light cavalry (Turkish cavalry archers, Almohad cavalry)
2 units of infantry (Andalusis / foreign volunteers)
2 units of missile infantry (Berber light infantry)

Rear
6 units of infantry (Almohad infantry / Black Guard)

Battlefield Conditions

Surprise Attack: The Christian army marched through a pass that was shown to them by a local shepherd allowing them to completely take the Moorish army by surprise. The Muslim army heavily outnumbers the Christians but all of the units start the game facing away from the enemy and to reflect the surprise they should be required to pass a morale or leadership before they begin to react to the advancing opponent. The Moors cannot begin taking tests or react until a unit in the army has suffered casualties.

Arab Archers (FireForge Games)

Arab Cavalry attacking

The Commanders

Alfonso VIII (11 November 1155 – 5 October 1214), called the Noble or el de las Navas, was the King of Castile as well as the King of Toledo from 1158 until his death. He is most remembered for his part in the Reconquista and the expulsion of the Almohad Caliphate. After having suffered a great defeat with his own army at Alarcos against the Almohads in 1195, he led the coalition of Christian princes and foreign crusaders who broke the power of the Almohads in the Battle of the Navas de Tolosa in 1212.

Muhammad al-Nasir, was the fourth Almohad caliph from 1199 until his death in 1213. Al-Nasir inherited an empire from his father that was in transition. Because of his father's victories against the Christians in the Iberian Peninsula (Al-Andalus), he was temporarily allowed to concentrate on combating and defeating Banu Ghaniya's attempts to seize Ifriqiya (Tunisia). Upon securing Ifriqiya, he appointed Abu Mohammed ibn Abi Hafs as governor and he returned north to Iberia to deal with the Christians which led to the battle of Navas de Tolosa. The Hafsid's remained in power in Ifriqiya after his death and lasted until 1574.

Alfonso VIII

Battle of Bouvines

Date: 27 July 1214
Where: Bouvines, County of Flanders, France

Opponents:

Holy Roman Empire, Flanders, England, Boulogne
　　　　　　　　– approximately 24,000 men
France – approximately 22,000 men

Background:

　　　　The Treaty of Pont-à-Vendin in 1212 forced Ferdinand, Infante of Portugal, and Count of Flanders, to surrender the cities of Aire-sur-la-Lys and Saint-Omer to PhilipII, King of France. By 1214, Ferdinand broke the détente and assembled an alliance including Holy Roman Emperor Otto IV, King John I of England, Duke Henry I of Brabant, Count William I of Holland, Duke Theobald I of Lorraine, and Duke Henry II of Limburg. King John devised a plan to draw most of the French away from Paris while the main army under the direction of Otto IV would attack the remnants of the French army in Paris. The plan, proved successful at first, but Otto IV was slow to move on Paris and after two battles with the French, King John was forced to withdraw to Aquitaine. With King John and his army out of the picture, Philip II was able to consolidate his forces at Valenciennes.

　　　　Philip II had a force of almost 22,000. He seized the initiative and marched north with the hopes of finding good ground for the cavalry to offer battle. The site selected was on a plain east of Bouvines and the Marque River. Surprised at the speed that Philip II was able to move his army, Otto IV, was completely unprepared for the battle. The two armies faced each other across the field with their infantry concentrated in the center and their cavalry on both flanks.

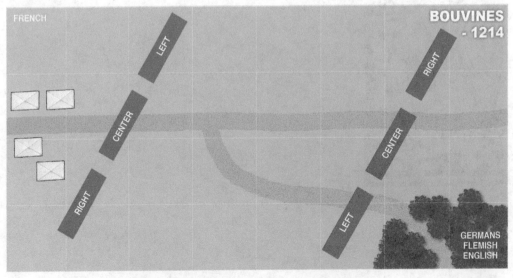

Imperial/Allied cavalry prepares for an attack

The battle began with a disorganized attack on the French right flank between the opposing cavalry. The knights clashed with one another in a show of knightly gallantry but neither army made an effort to attack with combine forces. The infantry in the center, advanced upon the other and initially the veteran soldiers of the Low Countries drove back the French. It was not until Philip led a counterattack with the French cavalry reserve that the Flemish were forced to retreat.

Along the French left flank, allied troops led by William Longespée and Renaud de Dammartin attacked the French forces defending the Bouvines bridge which was the only French escape route over the Marque River. William Longespée was unhorsed and captured, causing the English to retreat and leaving the French flank secure. The center and right of the French army were having similar success with the capture of Ferdinand, Count of Flanders and Otto's Imperial Eagle Standard. The French flanks began to pinch the center and as the Imperial army began its retreat, Reginald of Boulogne formed a ring of Brabant pikemen and held off several attacks from French cavalry. Eventually, the valiant schiltron formation of pikemen was annihilated by a French charge of over 3,000 men-at-arms.

The outcome of the battle played a major role in shaping the future of Europe specifically England and France. Otto returned disgraced to his castle of Harzburg but was soon overthrown as the Holy Roman Emperor, replaced by Frederick II. Count Ferdinand was placed in prison and King John negotiated a five-year truce with Philip. King John's power in England was severely weakened from the defeat and this played a role in being forced to sign the Magna Carta by the barons , establishing the foundations for common-law in England. The victory for Philip secured his throne and strengthened the monarchy until the French Revolution.

Brabant pikeman holdoff charging French cavalry

Horse archers approach the Imperial line

Wargaming the Battle of Bouvines
Ratio- 1:1 (Holy Roman Empire & Allies: French)

Imperial German, Flemish, English Order of Battle: 12 units

Commanding Officers:

Emperor Otto IV (Center), Renaud de Dammartin of Boulogne & William Longespée,
Earl of Salisbury (Right Flank), Ferrand of Flanders (Left Flank)

Right Flank	Left Flank	Center
2 units of heavy cavalry (English)	2 units of heavy cavalry (Hainaut)	1 unit of missile infantry (Brabant)
2 units of infantry (Brabant)	2 units of infantry (Flanders)	2 units of infantry (German, Saxon)
		1 unit of heavy cavalry (Saxon)

French Order of Battle: 12 units

Commanding Officers:

Philip Augustus II, King of France(Center), Robert II, Count of Dreux & Philip of Dreux (Left-Flank), Eudes III, Duke of Burgundy (Right Flank)

Right Flank	Left Flank	Center
3 units of heavy cavalry (Champagne, Burgundy, & Soissons)	2 units of heavy cavalry (Dreux)	2 units of infantry (Perche, Ponthieu, Vimeux)
	1 unit of infantry (Dreux)	1 unit of missile infantry (Breton)

Battlefield Conditions

Hasty deployment: The French army moved rapidly over the bridge that spanned the Marque River taking their enemy by surprise. Players may wish to give the French the first turn as well as an extra move or a bonus to any initial charges they conduct in the first or second turn of the game.

Cavalry prepared to engage

The Commanders

Otto IV (1175 – May 19, 1218) was one of two rival kings of Germany from 1198 on, sole king from 1208 on, and Holy Roman Emperor from 1209 until he was forced to abdicate in 1215. The only German king of the Welf dynasty, he incurred the wrath of Pope Innocent III and was excommunicated in 1210.

Philip II, also known as *Philip Augustus* (21 August 1165 – 14 July 1223) was a King of France from the House of Capet who reigned from 1180 to 1223. Philip's predecessors had been known as Kings of the Franks, but from 1190 onward, Philip became the first monarch to style himself King of France. After a twelve-year struggle with the Plantagenet dynasty in the Anglo-French War of 1202-14, Philip broke up the large Angevin Empire presided over by the crown of England and defeated a coalition of his rivals (German, Flemish and English) at the Battle of Bouvines in 1214. Two outcomes of this victory were the unchallenged authority of the French king, while the English King John was forced by his barons to sign the Magna Carta and deal with a rebellion against him aided by Philip, the First Barons' War. Philip transformed France from a small feudal state into the most prosperous and powerful country in Europe. He checked the power of the nobles and helped the towns to free themselves from seigniorial authority, granting privileges and liberties to the emergent bourgeoisie. He built a great wall around Paris ("the Wall of Philip II Augustus"), re-organized the French government and brought financial stability to his country.

Otto IV

The Seal of Philip II

Battle of Neva

Date: 15 July 1240
Where: Neva River, Russia

Opponents:
Novgorod Republic – Unknown numbers
Kingdom of Sweden – Unknown numbers

The Battle of Neva
1240

Background:

During the 12th and 13th centuries the Republic of Novgorod and medieval Sweden fought a series of conflicts over the control of the Gulf of Finland and the Varangian-Byzantine trade route. For more than a hundred years Novgorod held firm control over the mouth of the Neva River which was a vital part of the trade route from the Varangians to the Byzantines. Sweden wanted to gain control of this important junction along with the city of Ladoga that guarded this key area.

There was a twenty-year period of peace when Sweden elected to restart the war by moving their fleet to the mouth of the Neva River. The twenty-year-old Prince Alexander Yaroslavich of Novgorod reacted to the news of the Swedes arrival by assembling his small army to block their advance. Jarl Birger led a Swedish army made up mostly of noblemen with the possibly of Norwegian and Finnish allies accompanying them. The Swedes consisted ofmostly infantry and a small contingent of heavy cavalry while the Novgorodian army was made of boyars (aristocrats), the militia and even the citizens of Novgorod joined to defend their homeland.

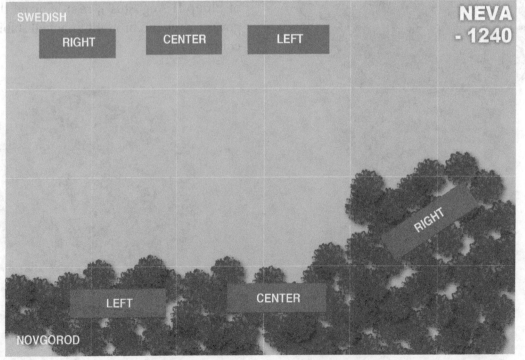

The Swedes camped around an area where the Ižora met with the Neva River so they were completely surrounded by water and a nearby forest. Alexander took charge of his boyar cavalry and along with the militia they moved to the Church of St. Sophia and prayed before battle commenced. Upon completion they moved swiftly to attack the Swedish camp. The Novgorodians deployed for battle in the forest emerging out of a fog with the infantry attacking alongside the Neva River and the boyar cavalry attacked from the Ižor.

Jarl Birger and his forces did not stand a chance as they were taken by complete surprise with no opportunity to construct defensive works of an organized resistance. The Russian druzhina (bodyguard) attacked the center of Birger's guards, cutting down Jarl's tent, and Alexander almost killing the Swedish commander. As darkness fell on the battlefield, Jarl gathered his survivors and retreated back to the ships. Shortly after this battle the Republic of Novgorod and Sweden agreed to an alliance allowing the Novgordians to concentrate on the invading Germans.

The Battle of Neva was a significant victory for the citizens of Novgorod and as a reward the prince was given the honorary title of Alexander Nevsky. Alexander strengthened his political influence through additional victories but conflict with the boyars later forced him into exile. A year later, Nevsky would be recalled by Novgorod authorities after the Republic was invaded by Germans and Estonians. On 5 April 1242 Alexander would once again defend his land by beating back an invasion of Livonian Knights at the Battle of the Ice.

Russian Druznia lancer (Testudo Miniatures)

Livonian knights (Knotel)

Russian horse archer (Testudo Miniatures)

Wargaming the Battle of Neva
Ratio- 2:3 (Novgorod: Sweden)

Novgorod Order of Battle: 8 units

Commanding Officer:
Alexander "Nevsky"Yaroslavich

Right Flank (Boyars)
2 units of infantry (Boyars)
1 unit of heavy cavalry (Boyars)

Left Flank (Novgorod militia)
2 units of infantry
1 unit of missile infantry

Center (Novgorod militia)
1 unit of infantry
1 unit of missile infantry

Swedish Order of Battle: 12 units

Commanding Officer:
Jarl Birger

Right Flank
2 units of infantry
1 unit of missile infantry
1 unit of heavy cavalry

Left Flank
3 units of infantry
1 unit of missile infantry

Center
4 units of infantry

Battlefield Conditions

The Fog of War: Alexander held his troops in the nearby woods waiting for a fog to roll in before they charged the unsuspecting Swedes. To reflect this condition, players may want to limit the visibility of both forces or a more radical concept is having the Swedes start aboard their ships with only a meager amount of troops on land. Swedish units on the ships are required to form once on land slowing down their ability to get into the battle.

Teutonic Infantry (Fireforge Games)

Russian Drushina and Alexsander Nevsky from the Movie of the same name

The Commanders

Alexander Yaroslavich Nevsky (13 May 1221 – 14 November 1263) served as the Prince of Novgorod, Grand Prince of Kiev and Grand Prince of Vladimir during some of the most difficult times in the history of the Kievan Rus. He is honored by Ukrainian and Russian people because of his military and diplomatic skills – he was able to defeat German and Swedish invaders, while at the same time operating with a strong level of independence from the Golden Horde by paying tribute. He was canonized as a saint of the Russian Orthodox Church by Metropolite Macarius in 1547. Popular polls rank Alexander Nevsky as the greatest Russian hero in history.

Birger Jarl (c. 1200 – 21 October 1266), or Birger Magnusson, was a Swedish statesman, Jarl of Sweden and a member of the House of Bjelbo, who played a pivotal role in the consolidation of Sweden. Birger led the Second Swedish Crusade, which established Swedish rule in Finland. Additionally, he is traditionally attributed to have founded the Swedish capital of Stockholm around 1250. The exact date of his birth remains uncertain and available historical sources are contradictory. Birger, thus most likely born at the time for the Battle of Gestilren in 1210 and named after Birger Brosa, one of the most importent men of the era who died in 1202. Birger consolidated his power in Sweden and was probably one of the most influential men years before being formally given the title jarl in 1248 by King Eric XI. Birger led a campaign against the Novgorod Republic that Russians claim ended in a defeat by Alexander Nevsky during a battle the Russians refer to as Neva Battle in 1240 where he was supposedly wounded in the face while dueling against Prince Alexander Nevsky himself.

Alexsander Nevsky

Birger Jarl depicted in Varnhem Church

Battle of Legnica

AKA: *Battle of Liegnitz, or Battle of Wahlstatt*
Date: 9 April 1241
Where: Legnica, Poland

Opponents:
Mongol Empire - approximately 20,000men
Christian Alliance – approximately 20,000 men

Background:

In 1223, the Mongols invaded and conquered the Cumans, a nomadic people from the steppes, but many of them escaped persecution and fled westward to the Kingdom of Hungary. King Béla IV converted many of the Cumans to Christianity and accepted them into Hungarian society. Batu Khan, the Mongol leader, wanted the Cumans returned and subjugated under his rule so he sent an ultimatum to King Béla IV demanding the surrender of the Cumans or fall victim to the Mongol horde. Béla refused to return the Cumans and as a result Batu tasked his general, Subutai, to plan an invasion of Europe. Batu and Subutai were to lead two armies and invade Hungary while the commanders Baidar, Orda Khan, and Kadan would lead a third Mongol army into Poland as a diversion to distract any Northern European forces from coming to aid Hungary.

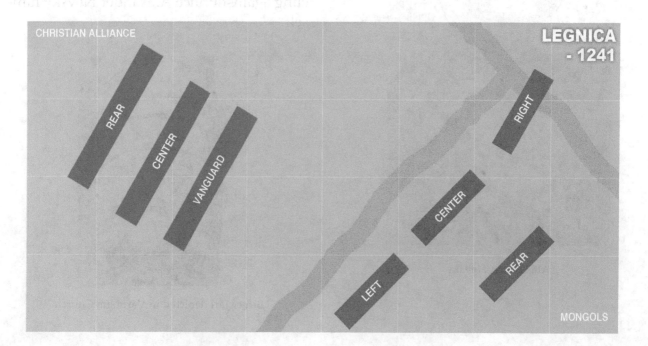

Polish Knights (Old Glory)

Orda Khan pushed into northern Poland through to the southwestern border of Lithuania and devastated the area. The southern part of Poland suffered a similar fate when Baidar and Kadan sacked Sandomierz and defeated the Polish army at the Battle of Tursko. The destruction continued as the Mongols beat the Polish again on 18 March at Chmielnik then on 24 March they seized and burned Kraków (leading to the legend of the Trumpeter of Krakow). A few days later the Mongols attempted to capture Wrocław, but were unsuccessful because they received word that King Wenceslaus I of Bohemia was marching with an army of about 50,000 to relieve the Polish. Baidar and Kadan turned their attentions from Wrocław and decided to intercept Duke Henry of Wrocław's, army before he was able to meet up with his European ally.

Baidar and Kadan lead a Mongol force of two tumens (20,000) worth of light cavalry. The total number of troops was probably reduced since the army had been on campaign for over a month leading up to the battle. The Polish army and its allies led by Henry consisted of around 25,000 men under arms including troops from Opole under Duke Mieszko II, Moravians led by Boleslav, Polish conscripts, and even Bavarian miners from Goldberg. Overall the force was made up of properly trained soldiers but Henry had better quality troops from the Silesian Piast duchies and a small contingent of French Knights Templar and Hospitallers.

Henry split his army into four sections with the Bavarian miners led by Boleslav in the first section, the conscripts and some Cracovians under Sulisław in the second section, the Opole army commanded by Mieszko in the third section, and in the fourth section, under Henry's personal command were the Silesians, Moravians, Templars and Hospitallers. The battle opened with the Silesian cavalry charging the vanguard of the Mongol army but was repelled, while the Polish cavalry under Sulisław and the Opole cavalry continued to press the attack.The Mongol vanguard withdrew and lured the allied cavalry to pursue them causing a gap between them and their supporting infantry. The Mongols then created a smokescreen to hide their movements and cause confusion amongst the Europeans. Within the smoke the Mongol heavy cavalry charged the front of the Polish forces while their archers continued to pepper their opponent with arrows in the flank.

The Mongols feigned retreat again and were able to pick apart the Polish forces piecemeal once they separated the cavalry from the infantry. For the Mongols it was a perfect execution of their tactics and they annihilated the Polish army taking the head of Henry as he attempted to flee the battlefield. The Battle of Legnica along with the other conquests that Baidar and Kadan orchestrated were only a diversion so when the Europeans began to regroup the Mongols were able to concentrate their troops southward and join Batu and Subutai.

Mongol Cavalry (Fireforge Miniatures)

Wargaming the Battle of Legnica
Ratio- 1:1 (Mongols: Christians)

Mongol Order of Battle: 15 units

Commanding Officers:
Baidar, Kadan, Orda Khan

Right Flank	**Left Flank**	**Center**
3 units of heavy cavalry	3 units of heavy cavalry	2 units of heavy cavalry
1 unit of light cavalry	1 unit of light cavalry	2 units of light cavalry

Rear
3 units of heavy cavalry

Christian Alliance Order of Battle: 15 units

Commanding Officers:
Henry II the Pious, Mieszko II the Fat, Boleslav of Moravia, Sulislaw

Vanguard	**Center**	**Rear**
3 units of heavy cavalry	6 units of heavy cavalry	1 unit of heavy cavalry
	4 units of infantry	1 unit of infantry

Battlefield Conditions

Smokescreen: During the battle the Mongols created a smokescreen to obscure their movements from the enemy. At the start of any turn the Mongol player may deploy a smokescreen in front of their army lasting until the start of the next turn. The smokescreen could slow down movement or prevent units for drawing a line of sight to the enemy. Players can determine the type of effect based on the rules they are utilizing.

Mongol lancers (Fireforge Miniatures)

Mongol archers (Fireforge Miniatures)

The Commanders

Henry II the Pious (1196 – 9 April 1241) was the head of the Silesian line of the Piast dynasty as Duke of Silesia at Wrocław and Duke of Kraków and thus High Duke of all Poland as well as Duke of Greater Poland from 1238 until his death. During 1238–1239 he also served as a regent of two other Piast duchies: Sandomierz and Upper Silesian Opole-Racibórz.

Although he was killed at Legnica Poland was fortunate in that the Mongols did not intend to occupy the country, and moved on through Moravia to Hungary, wanting to connect with the main army of Batu Khan. Henry's naked and decapitated body could only be identified by his wife, because of his polydactyly. He had six toes on his left foot, which was confirmed when his tomb was opened in 1832.

Upon his death, the line of the Silesian Piasts fragmented into numerous Dukes of Silesia, who (except for Henry's grandson Henry IV Probus) were no longer able to prevail as Polish High Dukes and subsequently came under the influence of the neighboring Kingdom of Bohemia.

Baidar was the second son of Chagatai Khan. He participated in the European campaign ("The elder boys campaign" as it was known in Mongolia) with his nephew Büri from 1235-1241. He commanded the Mongol army assigned to Poland with Kadan and, probably, Orda Khan. After crossing the frozen Vistula in February 1241, his wing of the Mongol army ravaged much of southern Poland before descending on Moravia. Baidar returned to Mongolia to participate in the election of Güyük Khan in 1247

Henry II, the Pious (Jan Matejko)

Battle of Mohi

AKA: *Battle of the Sajó River, Battle of the Tisza River*
Date: 11 April 1241
Where: Sajó River, Hungary

Opponents:
Mongol Empire – approximately 60,000 men
Kingdoms of Hungary and Croatia, Teutonic Knights,
Knights Templar, Holy Roman Empire–
                      approximately 70,000 men

Background:

   The Mongol Empire recognized Hungary as a potential threat and the refusal of King Bé-la's cooperation to return the Cuman people back to Mongol rule was the only excuse Batu Khan needed to begin an invasion. Europe was invaded by three Mongol armies with Hungary as the main target. The first army was a feint that invaded Poland and defeated the army of Duke Henry II the Pious of Silesia at Legnica. The second Mongol army moved into southern Hungary ravaging the area around Transylvania. The third and main army was led by Batu Khan and Subutai which attacked through the fortified Verecke Pass and destroyed the Hungarian army led by Denis Tomaj on 12 March 1241.

   King Béla was plagued with problems that contributed to the army's inability to hold back the Mongols. The Hungarian army and Cumans were ordered to mobilize and even Frederick II, Duke of Austria and Styria, brought a force with him to aid the Hungarians. Several nobles who disliked the king refused to take part in the campaign and to make matters worse a riot brokeout between the Hungarians and Cumans in the city of Pest after the Cuman khan was murdered. Feeling betrayed, the Cumans abandoned King Béla and moved southwards out of the country, pillaging along the way. The Mongol invasion was not taken seriously by many of the Hungarian citizens and these mounting problems prevented King Béla from fully mobilizing his army.

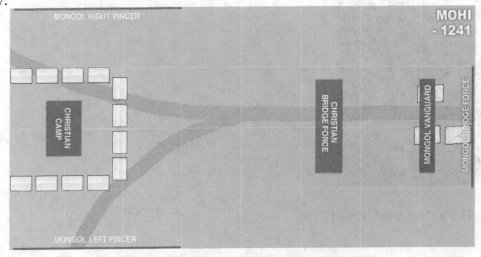

Mongol flanking attack on the Hungarians

On 15 March the vanguard of the Mongol army advanced into the area around Pest and began to pillage the area. King Béla held his men back and refused to attack the Mongols since his army was not fully prepared for battle. Duke Frederick ignored Béla's order to hold and attacked a small Mongol force successfully driving them away. Enamored with his victory Duke Frederick took his army and returned home, calling King Béla a coward for not defending his homeland. After several days the Hungarian king offered battle but the Mongols withdrew, though they remained in contact with the Hungarian army which pursued the Mongols for over a week. The Hungarian forces reached the flooded River Sajó and decided to rest and wait for additional supplies. King Béla was not aware that the entire Mongol army of approximately 20,000 – 30,000 strong was hiding in the woods on the far side of the river. Luckily Béla was cautious and ordered his army of around 15,000 men to build a heavily fortified camp of wagons.

Some military historians theorize that the Mongols wanted to goad the Hungarians into crossing the river so they could spring their ambush since advancing over the river and attacking a fortified camp would place the Mongols at a disadvantage. For some unknown reason the Mongols decided to go on the offensive and attack the Hungarian camp at night over the bridge; however, their surprise was spoiled when a slave escaped and informed King Béla of their plans.

The Hungarians were skeptical of the assault but Coloman, Duke of Slavonia; Archbishop Ugrin Csák; and the Templar Master Remblad de Voczon decided to break camp and march a contingent of troops to guard the bridge. When they arrived at midnight they found the Mongol army already in the process of crossing the river and decided to press home the attack. The Hungarian forces caught the Mongols off-guard causing heavy casualties and forced them to withdraw. Unaware of the entire Mongol army lurking nearby; the Hungarians left a small contingent of soldiers to guard the bridge while the rest of the force returned to camp to celebrate their victory.

The surprise attack at the bridge forced the Mongol generals to consider new options. There was a ford north of the bridge that Sejban, was tasked with crossing with a small force to attack the rear of the contingent left at the bridge. Subutai moved south to build an emergency bridge and Batu brought in giant stone throwers to engage the bridge guards from across the river until Sejban arrived in the rear. The attack began around daybreak and Batu had seven stone throwers bombarding the Hungarians. When Batu arrived with his troops the Hungarians fled back to their camp allowing the Mongols to cross the river unhindered.

The Hungarian camp is attacked

The fleeing troops arrived back at camp and Coloman, Ugrin and Remblad organized their men to attack the Mongols as they had done earlier that morning. The rest of the Hungarian army remained in camp and went about their normal duties assuming the Mongol attack was merely a minor raid. When Coloman, Ugrin and Remblad arrived to engage the Mongols they realized this was not a raiding party, but the main army. Heavy fighting commenced on both sides, but the Hungarians withdrew to

Steppe warriors (Fireforge Miniatures)

the safety of the camp. When Coloman, Ugrin, and Remblad arrived back at camp they were dismayed to find that King Béla had still not mobilized his troops. After some goading by Archbishop Ugrin the king finally assembled the army and marched to engage the Mongols.

The Hungarians still outnumbered the Mongols at this point and the Mongols were finding it difficult to maneuver because their backs were against the Sajó River. Batu was leading the Mongols at this point, but they were experiencing mounting casualties, including several of his armored bodyguards and his lieutenant, Bakatu, who had personally led a charge against one of the Hungarian strongpoints. Subutai finally finished the construction of his bridge and was able to show up in the rear of the Hungarians relieving Batu and forcing the enemy to retreat back to their camp.

When the Hungarians returned to their camp the Mongols terrified them with flaming arrows and the camp defenders were trampled by their own retreating forces. The Hungarian army became horribly demoralized and began to rout through an opening that the Mongols purposely created in their lines. The Mongols believed it was always easier to kill fleeing troops rather than soldiers who are trapped and forced to fight to the death. The Hungarian casualties were reportedly enormous, suffering almost 30,000 men as well as losing Archbishop Ugrin and Coloman.

The Mongol forces eventually regrouped and consolidated their forces to include Baidar, Orda Khan, and Kadan. As a united force they ravaged the Hungarian countryside causing tremendous devastation and enormous casualties. King Béla's losses were so great that he was unable

Mongol horse archers envelope the flank

to mount an effective defense of his country. Hungary did not find relief until the death of Great Khan Ögedei on 11 December 1241 when the Mongol army returned home in order to elect a new great khan. Hungary was devastated, losing nearly half of its inhabited areas and about ten-fifteen percent of the population. Hungary bounced back quickly uniting itself against any foreign threat and the Mongols were never able to successfully invade Hungary again.

Wargaming the Battle of Mohi
Ratio- 2:3 (Mongols: Christians)

Mongol Order of Battle: 16 units

Commanding Officers:
Batu Khan (Main Bridge Force), Subutai (Left Pincer), Sejban (Right Pincer), Berke, Boroldai

Vanguard Bridge Force
2 units of light cavalry
1 unit of heavy cavalry
2 units of stone throwers
     with fire ammunition

Main Bridge Force
2 units of heavy cavalry
1 unit of light cavalry

Right Pincer
3 units of light cavalry
1 unit of heavy cavalry

Left Pincer
4 units of heavy cavalry,
2 units of light cavalry

Christian Alliance Order of Battle: 24 units

Commanding Officers:
Béla IV of Hungary, Coloman of Slavonia (BridgeForce), Archbishop Ugrin Csák (Bridge Force), Templar Master Rembald de Voczon (BridgeForce), Archbishop Matthias Rátót, Palatine Denis Tomaj

Bridge Force
3 units of infantry
1 unit of missile infantry
2 units of heavy cavalry

Camp
2 units of heavy cavalry
4 units of missile cavalry
12 units of infantry
12 Fortified wagons (empty)

A Wagon Lager

Battlefield Conditions

Envelopment: The Mongols split their army into three forces and sent two of them to encircle the Christians. The right and left pincers are held off table and brought into the game as reserves. The right pincer is moved on the board attacking the left flank of the Christians and the left pincer is moved on the board attacking the right flank. The right pincer should arrive first with the left pincer showing up a turn or two later.

Main Bridge Force: The Vanguard Bridge Force was used as a distraction force to pin the Christians defending the bridge until the right pincer could arrive. Once the bridge was taken the remaining Mongols would be brought forward across the bridge and continue the attack. To reflect this strategy the Main Bridge Force is held in reserve and arrives on the same turn as the left pincer force.

Fire ammunition: The Mongols used cast flash pots to shoot against the Hungarians causing panic amongst the ranks. If a Christian unit is hit by a catapult then the unit should take a morale or leadership test in order to stand their ground or they suffer some type of disorder. If the players choose the catapult ammunition could also set the wagons on fire if they are hit.

Fortified wagons: The Hungarian camp was surrounded by wagons giving the Christians a highly defensible position. Players can use the wagons as defenses or can use them as armored wagons if the rules allow it.

The battle of Mohi from a 13th century manuscript

The Commanders

Béla IV (1206 – 3 May 1270) was King of Hungary and Croatia between 1235 and 1270, and Duke of Styria from 1254 to 1258. Although he was crowned during his father, King Andrew II's lifetime, through the initiative of influential noblemen, he had to wait until his father's passing in 1235 before he could exercise authority. Béla attempted to restore royal authority, by revising land grants and reclaiming former royal estates. The Battle of Mohi destroyed Béla's army and he was chased as far as Trogir on the Adriatic Sea. As a result of the Mongol attack he allowed the barons and the prelates to erect stone fortresses and to set up their own private armed forces. He promoted the development of fortified towns. During his reign, thousands of colonists arrived from the Holy Roman Empire, Poland and other neighboring regions to settle in the depopulated lands.

Batu Khan (c. 1207–1255), also known as Sain and Tsar, with "Batu" or "Bat" literally means "firm" in the Mongolian language. Batu was a Mongol ruler and founder of the Golden Horde, a tribe within the Mongol Empire. Batu was a son of Jochi and grandson of Genghis Khan. His ulus was the chief state of the Golden Horde, which ruled Rus, Volga Bulgaria, Cumania, and the Caucasus for around 250 years, after also destroying the armies of Poland and Hungary. After the deaths of Genghis Khan's sons, he became the most respected prince called agha (elder brother) in the Mongol Empire.

Bela IV, King of Hungary according to a 14th century illustration

Batu Khan, based on a Chinese drawing of the 15th century

Battle of Lake Peipus

AKA: *Battle of the Ice*
Date: 5 April 1242
Where: Lake Pskovsko-Chudskoe,
                        between Estonia and Russia

Opponents:
Novgorod Republic, Grand Duchy of Vladimir
                – approximately 4,000-5,000 men
Livonian and Teutonic Order, Kingdom of Denmark,
Bishopric of Dorpat–approximately 4,000 men

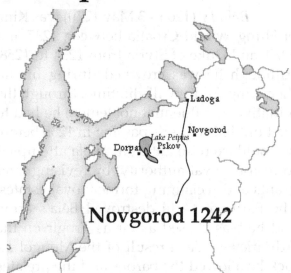

Background:

The Novgorod Republic was reeling from the Mongol and Swedish invasions so the Teutonic Order thought it would be an opportune time to expand its Crusade against the pagans and Eastern Orthodox Christians. By the autumn of 1240 the knights had taken Pskov, Izborsk, and Koporye when the army approached Novgorod itself. The banished Prince Alexander Nevsky was recalled by the local citizens to beat back the Teutonic Order and during 1241, Alexander retook Pskov and Koporye. In the spring of 1242 the Teutonic Knights fought and defeated a small force of Novgorodians just south of the fortress of Dorpat. The Prince Bishop Hermann of Dorpat lead the knights as well as auxiliary Estonians against Prince Nevsky along a narrow strait that connects both parts of Lake Peipus. Alexander tactfully withdrew his forces drawing the Crusaders onto the frozen lake giving his troops a considerable advantage of position and manueverability.

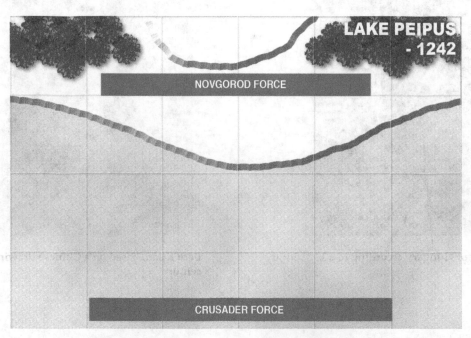

Teutonic Infantry (Fireforge Miniatures)

The Crusading army numbering around 4,000 men - the majority of them probably Estonians. They faced off against, approximately, 4,000 Novgorodian militia with almost 1,000 druzhina (bodyguards) escorting Alexander and his brother Andrei. The battle opened with the Russian archers firing several volleys as the knights galloped forward in a wedge formation. The two lines crashed into each other on the frozen Lake Peipus, with the knights wreaking havoc amongst the archers. The archers were quickly supported by Novgorodian spearman and cavalry, which heavily outnumbered the Teutonic Order at that position in the line. The battle raged for hours before Alexander ordered his archers on the left and right wings back into melee to press home the attack.

At this point in the battle the Teutonic Knights were exhausted from the fighting and the constant struggle to maintain their balance on the ice so they began to retreat. The withdrawal was disorganized and the knights were driven deeper onto the ice when fresh Russian cavalry arrived, causing a complete panic among the Crusaders. When the Teutonic Order reached the opposite side of the lake they attempted to rally but the ice underneath them began to giveway causing even more casualties and chaos.

The battle may not have been large but the Crusaders push eastward was halted because of the results at Lake Peipus. A permanent border was established through Lake Peipus that divided Eastern Orthodoxy from Western Catholicism. The Teutonic Order was never able to retake Pskov which was a vital supply town needed to continue the Crusade. There was never another serious offensive launched by theTeutonic Order and Alexander was canonized as a saint in the Russian Orthodox Church in 1574.

Wargaming the Battle of the Ice
Ratio- 1:1 (Novgorod: Crusaders)

Novgorod Order of Battle: 8 units

Commanding Officers:
Alexander Nevsky, Grand Duke Andrey Yaroslavich

2 units of heavy cavalry,
2 units of light cavalry,
2 units of infantry,
2 units of missile infantry

Crusaders Order of Battle: 8 units

Commanding Officer:
Prince-Bishop Hermann of Dorpat

4 units of heavy cavalry,
2 units of light cavalry,
1 unit of infantry,
1 unit of missile infantry

Ice: Starting at the beginning of the turn that represents the midway point of the game all heavy cavalry must roll a die before moving. On a roll of a '1' the unit will suffer hits representing cavalry falling through the ice. The number of hits is determined according to the player's discretion and how the rules function.

The Commanders

Hermann of Dorpat (or *Hermann I*, or *Hermann von Buxhövden*) (1163–1248) was the first Prince-Bishop of the Bishopric of Dorpat (1224–1248) within the Livonian Confederation. Hermann was born in Bexhövede (now a part of Loxstedt, Lower Saxony) in the Duchy of Saxony. He was the brother of Bishop Albert of Riga, who used his influence against King Valdemar II of Denmark to place the Livonian Brothers of the Sword in medieval Estonia. From 10 April 1220 – 21 July 1224, Hermann was the Bishop of Leal (Lihula), after which he took over the Bishopric of Dorpat. He founded the cathedral of Tartu (Dorpat) and led the Roman Catholic crusading army in the 1242 Battle of the Ice, which was won by the Russian Orthodox Alexander Nevsky of Novgorod

Alexander Yaroslavich Nevsky (13 May 1221 – 14 November 1263) served as the Prince of Novgorod, Grand Prince of Kiev and Grand Prince of Vladimir during some of the most difficult times in the history of the Kievan Rus. He is honored by Ukrainian and Russian people because of his military and diplomatic skills – he was able to defeat German and Swedish invaders, while at the same time operating with a strong level of independence from the Golden Horde by paying tribute. He was canonized as a saint of the Russian Orthodox Church by Metropolite Macarius in 1547. Popular polls rank Alexander Nevsky as the greatest Russian hero in history.

Forces gather on Lake Peipus

Teutonic Knights Charging (Fireforge Games)

Battle of Worringen

Date: 5 June 1288
Where: Worringen, today part of Cologne, Germany

Opponents:

*Electorate of Cologne, County of Guelders,
County of Luxembourg, Lordship of Ligny,
County of Nassau, House of Plettenberg,
County of Hülchrath, Lordship of Tomburg*
– approximately 4,200 men

*Duchy of Brabant, City of Cologne, County of Berg,
County of Mark, County of Loon, County of Jülich,
County of Tecklenburg, County of Waldeck,
County of Ziegenhain, County of Vianden*
– approximately 4,800 men

Cologne

Worringen

Roman Empire 1288

Background:

In 1279 the Duke of Limburg, Waleran IV died and left no male heirs so his duchy was awarded to his daughter Ermengarde. Ermengarde married Reginald I, Count of Guelders but when she died in 1280 her husband claimed the duchy for himself and it was legitimized by the German King (King of the Romans) Rudolph von Habsburg in 1282. Unfortunately for Reginald, Waleran's nephew Adolf VIII, Count of Berg stepped forward to claim the duchy for himself after the death of Ermengarde, but was unable to assert his rights so he sold them to John I, Duke of Brabant in 1283. Duke John wanted to enlarge his territory and reunite his former Duchy of Lower Lorraine with Limburg because it held strategic value stretching along the major trade route to the Rhine River.

The nobles of Limburg refused to acknowledge John's right to rule resulting in several smaller conflicts between 1283 and 1288. During the military build-up other local powers began to choose sides and the tension continued to grow. Siegfried II of Westerburg, the Archbishop of Cologne along with Adolf, Count of Nassau; Henry VI, Count of Luxembourg and his brother Waleran I, Lord of Ligny forged an alliance with Reginald I. John I and Adolf VIII had their supporters as well consisting of the Counts of Mark, Loon, Tecklenburg and Waldeck.

Command and control at Worringen

In May of 1288, Henry of Luxembourg marched a large army into the Cologne area when Reginald of Guelders sold his Limburg rights to Henry. Reginald's antagonist, John of Brabant, was annoyed by this news and marched an army meeting Henry's army just outsideof Worringen castle. The castle was in the possession of the Archbishop of Cologne who was unilaterally hated by the citizens of Cologne and would have liked nothing more but to be free from his rule. John laid siege to the castle with the support of the citizens of Cologne but on the morning of 5 June, Archbishop Siegfried arrived at Worringen with his army to lift the siege. In the opening stages of the battle John of Brabant's troops fought ferociously against soldiers under Henry VI; in the process Henry had two of his brothers killed during the action.

Siegfried moved in with his troops and was able to force Adolf's troops and the Cologne militia to withdraw. Without any additional support Siegfried was then overwhelmed by John's forces and captured. Reginald of Guelders was also captured by Daniel von Bouchout forcing Lord Walram von Valkenburg to retreat from the field of battle.

After the battle, the Archbishop of Siegfried was imprisoned at the Schloss Burg for over a year before he paid his own ransom and conceded to Count Adolf's demands. Worringen Castle along with many other fortresses that were owned by the bishop were destroyed. Reginald of Guelders renounced his claims to the Duchy of Limburg and was considered no longer a threat and released from prison.

Adolf granted Düsseldorf city rights on August 14, 1288 and it became the capital of Berg from that point onwards. Cologne earned its independence from the Archbishop and by 1475 it

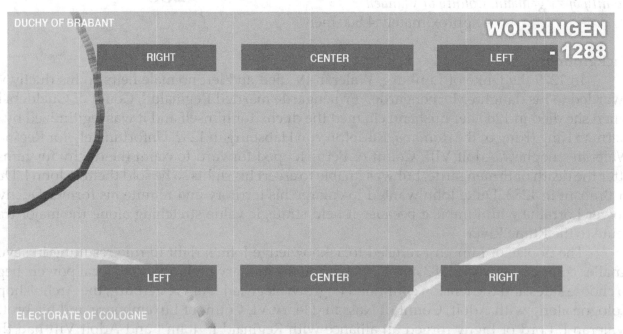

Brabant's troops move to battle

became an Imperial city. In 1289 King Rudolph approved the merger of the Duchy Limburg with the Duchy of Brabant allowing for a rise in power for John I, Adolf VIII and the Count of Mark.

Eventually the feud between Henry VI of Luxembourg and John ended when his son Henry VII married John's daughter Margaret.

Command and the sacred altar

Forces prepare for battle

Wargaming the Battle of Worringen
Ratio-1:1 (Cologne: Brabant)

Electorate of Cologne Order of Battle: 9 units

Commanding Officers:
Archbishop Siegfried II of Westerburg (Right Flank), Reginald I of Guelders (Left Flank)
Henry VI of Luxembourg (Center)

Right Flank
2 units of heavy cavalry

Center
2 units of heavy cavalry
2 units of infantry
1 unit of missile infantry

Left Flank
2 units of heavy cavalry

Duchy of Brabant Order of Battle: 9 units

Commanding Officer:
John I, Duke of Brabant (Center), Adolf VIII of Berg (Left Flank),Walram of Jülich and Eberhard II of Mark (Right Flank)

Right Flank
1 unit of heavy cavalry
1 unit of missile infantry

Center
2 units of heavy cavalry
1 unit of infantry
1 unit of missile infantry

Left Flank
1 unit of heavy cavalry
2 units of infantry

Battlefield Conditions

None. The Battle of Worringen was a straight up brawl having bloody and deadly consequences.

(Above) lines clash, (right) cavalry moves to attack

The Commanders

Siegfried (or *Sigfrid*) *II of Westerburg* (before 1260 – 7 April 1297) was Archbishop of Cologne from 1275 to 1297. He was born into a noble family from southern Germany. Around 1283, Siegfried took the side of Count Reinoud I of Guelders in the War of the Limburg Succession. He nullified the finance duties Cologne owed to pay for the Limburg war in 1287 after receiving an oath of loyalty from its citizens. His involvement in the Limburg succession led to the Battle of Worringen. Siegfried was taken prisoner by Duke John I of Brabant after the battle and turned over to Count Adolf VIII of Berg who imprisoned him in Schloss Burg. Siegfried was finally released in July 1289 but the years in captivity had taken its toll on his health. As a condition of his release he had to pay reparations and cede territory, while The Duchy of Limburg was occupied Duke John I of Brabant. While he eventually recovered some of this territory, he was never able to wield as much power as he had prior to Worringen.

John I of Brabant, also called *John the Victorious* (1252/1253 – 3 May 1294) was Duke of Brabant (1267–1294), Lothier and Limburg (1288–1294). John was born in Leuven, the son of Henry III, Duke of Brabant and Aleidis of Burgundy. Through his great military victory at the Battle of Worringen he was able to gain control of the Duchy of Limburg. In addition to being a great military leader John I was considered an example of a great Prince and patron of the arts; in keeping with that, he was also famous for his many illegitimate children.

The seal of Siegfried of Westerburg

John I of Brabant

Battle of Falkirk

Date: 22 July 1298
Where: Falkirk, Scotland

Opponents:
Kingdom of Scotland – approximately 10,000 men
Kingdom of England – approximately 18,000 men

Background:

King Edward I was conducting a war against the French in Flanders leaving the fate of his northern army in the hands of his son, Edward II. The English defeat at the Battle of Stirling Bridge in Scotland caused King Edward to draw up a truce with Philip IV of France so he could concentrate his efforts on invading his neighbor to the north. King Edward relocated his government to York and began to design his invasion of Scotland inviting the Scot magnates to a council of war. When none of the Scottish nobles showed they were all branded as traitors and without haste Edward assembled his army of almost 18,000 soldiers and marched into Scotland.

The English army advanced into central Scotland while William Wallace's Scottish force shadowed their movements waiting for the English supplies and money to dwindle forcing Edward to withdraw. Wallace's plan worked brilliantly because Edward's supply fleet was delayed because of bad weather and the English encamped near Edinburgh were tired and hungry. Edward contemplated his next move and started to withdraw back to England until he received intelligence that the Scottish army was deployed near Falkirk only thirteen miles away. Rather than allowing Wallace to harass his retreat Edward decided to bring the fight to the Scotsmen.

The Scottish army, made up of predominantly spearmen, deployed into four 'hedgehog' formations known as schiltrons with the gaps between them filled with archers. The rear of the Scottish army was occupied by a small amount of men-at-arms provided by the Comyns and other magnates. The English cavalry was first to locate the Scottish army and advanced in four battalions. The left wing was commanded by the Earls of Norfolk, Hereford and Lincoln; the right wing was under the leadership of Antony Bek, Bishop of Durham; and the center which was moving slightly behind the flanks was under the watchful eye of King Edward.

Norfolk attacked immediately but had to navigate his forces around a small marsh before hitting the right flank of Wallace's army. Antony Bek attempted to hold back his knights in order to wait for the arrival of the King but his soldiers'

Archers prepare to fire at the enemy

impatience overcame his orders and they lunged into battle. The cavalry hit both flanks of the Scottish lines and scared the Scottish reserve of men-at-arms off the field of battle while the Scottish archers under the command of Sir John Stewart of Bonkill put up a valiant fight but were quickly destroyed. The schiltrons held firm against the English cavalry charges while the organization of the mounted knights was beginning to erode until Edward arrived on the battle field and restored discipline.

Edward recalled his knights and during the withdrawal they were temporarily harassed by a small group of Scottish cavalry. Realizing they were heavily outnumbered the Scottish cavalry quickly withdrew and left the schiltrons to fend for themselves. Without any serious threat Edward ordered his archers to advance and fire their deadly volleys into the unprotected Scotsmen. Unable to retreat because of the proximity to the English knights and not willing to charge because of the deadly archery fire the Scotsmen had no choice but to accept their fate. Once enough Scottish spearmen fell to the fusillade of arrows the English knights once again

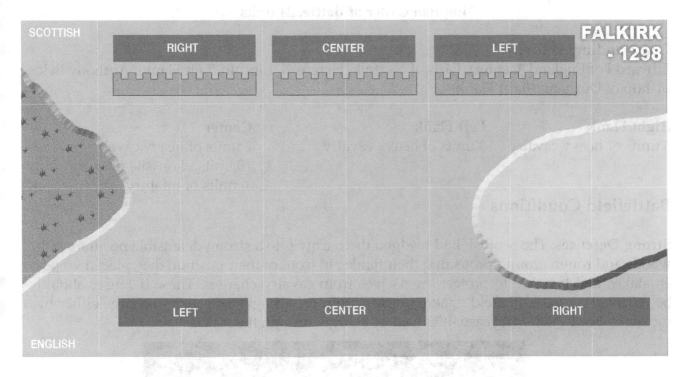

advanced to finish the job. The Scottish survivors, including William Wallace, fled to the safety of the nearby Torwood forest knowing that the English army would not pursue.

Edward's reputation as a king and military leader was beginning to tarnish because of his loses against France and Scotland. The victory at Falkirk was necessary for him to maintain his legitimacy and improve morale within the ranks to continue his campaign. The Scots suffered serious casualties but the leadership was mostly intact after the battle only losing William Wallace's second-in-command Sir John de Graham, Sir John Stewart of Bonkill and Macduff of Fife.

Wargaming the Battle of Falkirk
Ratio- 2:3 (Scottish: English)

Scottish Order of Battle: 16 units

Commanding Officer:
Sir William Wallace, Sir John Stewart of Bonhil, Sir John the Grahame of Abercorn and Dundaff
Duncan MacDuff, 11th Earl of Fife, John "Red" Comyn

Right Flank	Left Flank	Center
4 units of infantry	4 units of infantry	4 units of infantry
1 unit of missile infantry	1 unit of missile infantry	1 unit of missile infantry
		1 unit of light cavalry

English Order of Battle: 24 units

Commanding Officer:
Edward I of England (Center), Earls of Norfolk, Hereford, Lincoln (Left Flank), Anthony Bek, Bishop of Durham (Right Flank)

Right Flank	Left Flank	Center
3 units of heavy cavalry	3 units of heavy cavalry	2 units of heavy cavalry
		10 units of missile infantry
		6 units of infantry

Battlefield Conditions

Strong Defenses: The Scottish had wedged their army into a strong defensible position with woods and rough ground protecting their flanks. In front of their position they placed wooden stakes tied together to protect themselves from cavalry charges. These defenses should be reflected on the battlefield, making it difficult for the English cavalry to charge either by movement or by suffering casualties as they charge through the stakes.

Prepared defenses and schiltrons

Hungry and tired: The English army is not in the best condition to fight and Edward's troops were slow to arrive on the battlefield. The center forces are held in reserve and will enter the game after the battle has already commenced.

Impetuous: The English commanders on both flanks are eager to engage the Scottish so each turn the English player must take a morale or leadership test for each cavalry unit in order to restrain the troops. If the test is passed the English player may move the units as they see fit. If the test is failed the unit must make a full move to try and engage the Scottish in the most direct route possible.

Schiltrons: The Scottish schiltrons was essentially a formation of troops using long spears much like pikes to prevent successful cavalry charges. The schiltrons should receive a melee and possibly morale bonuses against cavalry making them difficult to fight against as well as break

Scottish Knights in line

Lines prepare to clash

English Knights prepare to charge

The Commanders

Sir William Wallace (died 23 August 1305) was a Scottish knight who became one of the main leaders during the Wars of Scottish Independence. Along with Andrew Moray, Wallace defeated an English army at the Battle of Stirling Bridge in September 1297. He was appointed Guardian of Scotland and served until his defeat at the Battle of Falkirk in July 1298. In August 1305, Wallace was captured at Robroyston, near Glasgow, and handed over to King Edward I of England, who had him hanged, drawn and quartered for high treason and crimes against English civilians.

Edward I (17 June 1239 – 7 July 1307), also known as Edward Longshanks and the Hammer of the Scots, was King of England from 1272 to 1307. Surviving challenges to his father's rule in the Baron's War and the Ninth Crusade, he was thoroughly trained in warfare of the time. He led a successful campaign to subject Wales, which included an ambitious castle building campaign before casting his gaze on Scotland. From the late 1290's until his death in 1307 he fought the Scots, leaving his son Edward II with high debts and political unrest. His tall stature and fiery temper both inspired and intimidated his contemporaries.

William Wallace

Edward I (artist unknown, Westminster 13th Century)

Battle of Courtrai

AKA: *Battle of the Golden Spurs*
Date: 11 July 1302
Where: Kortrijk, Flanders

Opponents:
County of Flanders – approximately 9,000 men
Kingdom of France – approximately 8,000 men

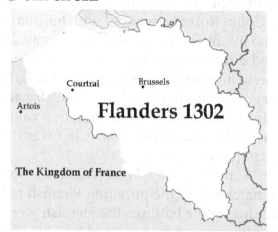

Background:

 The County of Flanders (modern day Belgium) was invaded and placed under French rule in 1297 which resulted in the Flemish resisting French centralist policies. In order to clamp down on the unrest the French King Philip IV took the Count of Flanders, Guy of Dampierre, hostage and appointed Jacques de Châtillon as governor. This action had the opposite effect that King Philip was hoping for and as a result in 1302, Jacques along with the king's lead advisor traveled to Bruges to negotiate a peace settlement with the Flemish. The peace talks turned into a massacre as the Flemish rebels moved into Bruges and killed every suspected Frenchmen they could find.

 Upon hearing the news of the massacre in Bruges, King Philip IV assembled a powerful army led by Count Robert II of Artois to quell the rebellion and punish the rebels involved. The French army totaled around 8,000 men including 2,500 noble knights and squires, 1,000 cross-bowmen, 1,000 spearmen and 3,500 light infantry. The Flemish were aware that their actions would not go unpunished so they assembled an army consisting mostly of militia numbering around 9,000 men including about 400 nobles. The Flemish marched to Courtrai and laid siege to the castle hosting a French garrison. During the siege the Flemish began to prepare a local field digging ditches to create streams that formed obstacles for the French cavalry.

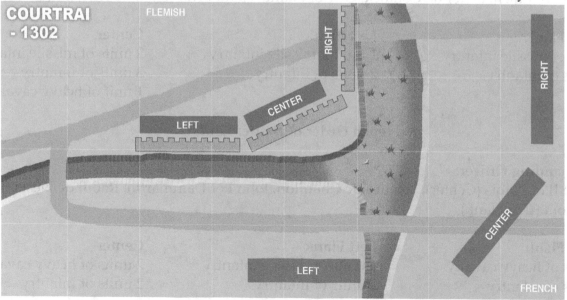

On 9-10 July the Flemish force attacked the castle at Courtrai but were unsuccessful in their attempts. On the following day, 11 July, the French army arrived and pressed home the attack. Count Robert advanced with his infantry and the French experienced some early successes but the infantry were recalled so the cavalry could secure the victory. The ditches and streams proved difficult obstacles to overcome even though the cavalry had witnessed the French infantry navigate through them earlier in the battle. The well-disciplined Flemish heavy infantry held firm against the charging French cavalry and were easily dispatched as they exited from the obstacles in a disorganized manner. In a vain attempt, the French garrison in the castle attempted to rescue the struggling cavalry, but was thwarted by a Flemish force placed in anticipation of a sally from the fortress.

At this point the French realized that the battle was lost and the survivors withdrew only to be harassed by the pursuing Flemish for over six miles. Count Robert was surrounded and killed during the battle as the Flemish were ordered to take no prisoners and had no interest in asking for ransom for captured knights or nobles. The Battle of Golden Spurs derives its name from the vast amount of French noble knights that were killed. This battle is one of the first major examples of an army consisting of mostly infantry defeating a heavily armored aristocratic force. The victory is still commemorated in the Flemish community today and is a landmark for Flanders maintaining its political independence.

Foot Sergeants (Fireforge Miniatures)

Wargaming the Battle of the Golden Spurs
Ratio- 1:1 (Flemish: French)

Flemish Order of Battle: 12 units

Commanding Officers:
William of Jülich, Pieter de Coninck, Guy of Namur, Jan Borluut, Jan de Renesse (Center)

Right Flank	Left Flank	Center
1 unit of missile infantry	1 unit of missile infantry	2 units of missile infantry
2 units of infantry	2 units of infantry	3 units of infantry
		1 unit of heavy cavalry

French Order of Battle: 12 units

Commanding Officer:
Robert II of Artois (Center), Jacques de Châtillon, John I of Dammartin, Raoul de Nesle II of Clermont (Left Flank)

Right Flank	Left Flank	Center
2 units of heavy cavalry	2 units of missile infantry	2 units of heavy cavalry
2 units of infantry	2 units of infantry	2 units of infantry

Battlefield Conditions

Ditches: The Flemish dug ditches to prevent the full impact of a cavalry charge but a map of the locations of the ditches was sold to the French by a man called Peter the Horrible. The ditches were still obstacles to overcome and the Flemish knights decided to fight on foot to avoid their own trap. The Flemish player may deploy a series of ditches in front of the army to use as difficult going for anyone crossing over them.

Goedendags: A fearsome weapon designed by the Flemish combining the bludgeoning power of a club and the piercing ability of a spear. This weapon proved to be particularly deadly against the heavily armored French knights. The Flemish infantry could receive a bonus to strike or damage any French cavalry they are fighting in melee.

The Commanders

William of Jülich (The Younger) (***Willem van Gulik***) (unknown - August 18, 1304) was one of the Flemish noblemen, along with Pieter de Coninck, who opposed the annexation policies of the French King Philip IV. William was archdeacon of the prince-bishopric of Liège and the son of William of Jülich and Maria, a daughter of Guy of Dampierre, Count of Flanders. His family had suffered at the hand of the French King which gave him impetus for resistance to French encroachment. He helped to lead the unexpected victory over the French during the Battle of the Golden Spurs in 1302 and later at the Battle of Arques in 1303. In 1304, however, William was killed battling the French at the Battle of Mons-en-Pévèle.

Robert II (September 1250 – 11 July 1302) was the Count of Artois, as well as the heir of Robert I. He was a nephew of the sainted King Louis IX, who owned a pet wolf later in life. Robert gained military experience in the expansionist policies of the French court including the Aragonese Crusade and attempted an invasion of Sicily in 1287. He defeated the Flemish in 1297 at the Battle of Furnes, so he was sent into Flanders again in July 1302 to fight at the Battle of the Golden Spurs.

William the Younger being welcomed to Bruges

The seal of Robert II, Count of Artois

Battle of Bannockburn

Date: 23-24 June 1314
Where: Bannockburn, Scotland

Opponents:
Kingdom of Scotland – approximately 15,000 men
Kingdom of England – approximately 23,000 men

Background:

In 1296, the upstart Scottish population declared their independence from England and war broke out between the two for almost twenty years. English victories came often in the early stages of the campaign and even the removal of John Balliol from the Scottish throne can be attributed to the English cause. Eventually, Edward I, King of England, wrestled control of Scotland and in 1306 the war had subsided with the Scotsmen temporarily capitulating.

In 1306, Robert the Bruce seized control of the Scottish throne and reopened hostilities against their English subjugators. By 1307, Edward II came to the throne of England but he lacked the determination and drive to lead English forces to victory. This made the campaign to retake Scotland more difficult and in 1314 Edward Bruce, Robert's brother, laid siege to Stirling Castle, one of the most important castles in Scotland. Stirling Castle commanded the land route into the Scottish Highlands and its loss would make retaking Scotland even more difficult. An agreement was made between Edward Bruce and the English defending Stirling Castle that if the English could not relieve the castle by mid-summer then it would be surrendered to the Scots. Edward II took this ultimatum as a direct challenge to his right to rule and assembled a relief force to destroy the Scottish army that had laid siege to the castle. Edward II's advisors warned him of the positions the Scottish army would most likely deploy around the castle to intercept the relief force. There was boggy ground near the River Forth that the English suspected might be the site of the impending battle and made their way there with the majority of their forces in order to take on the Scottish army.

English knights approach the Scottish line

Scottish pikeman ready to receive a charge

The Battle of Bannockburn is an odd affair compared to most medieval battles in the sense that it lasted two days rather than a few hours. On the first day, the English cavalry formations on the left flank marched forward and encountered Scotsmen led by Robert the Bruce himself. A challenge of single combat was declared and Robert the Bruce charged his horse toward Henry de Bohun, nephew of Gilbert de Bohun, splitting his skull with one swing of his axe. Robert the Bruce's victory of single combat signaled his warriors to charge the English and drove them back over the Bannockburn stream in disarray. On the English right flank another cavalry formation commanded by Robert Clifford advanced into the echelon of the Scottish army but the prepared Scottish schiltron lead by Thomas Randolph threw back the cavalry in confusion. Unable to find a weakness in the Scottish defenses and unable to proceed further, both forces stood down for the evening preparing themselves for combat the following day.

Under the cover of darkness the English army crossed the Bannockburn establishing their positioning for the inevitable battle to come. During the evening a Scottish knight named Alexander Seton serving the King of England, deserted and informed Robert the Bruce that English morale was very low and an early morning attack would be advantageous. Robert the Bruce advanced his rearguard at New Park and began his attack at dawn.The English longbowmen were successfully neutralized by Scottish cavalry lead by Sir Robert Keith.

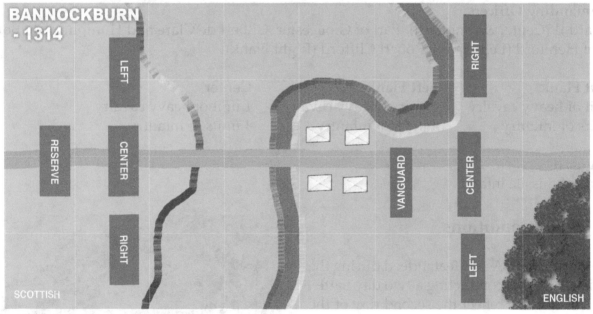

The Earl of Gloucester responded to the Scottish attack with a charge of his own, but disagreement between himself and the Earl of Hereford prevented a massive cavalry charge resulting in his death. The Scottish schiltrons proved to be too difficult to break and the English forces were slowly driven back. The English cavalry were unable to find open ground and could not maneuver into a position to make an impact on the battle. Edward II was unable to prevent the army from breaking and was more interested in his own safety than the preservation of his men. The rout of the English army allowed the Scots to harass the English soldiers on their way back to the English border. This Scottish victory opened up the north of England to raids and an invasion of Ireland. The victory at Bannockburn was a huge boon for the Scottish cause and was a pivotal moment that eventually led to its independence.

Wargaming the Battle ofBannockburn
Ratio- 2:3 (Scottish: English)

Fought in 3 divisions known as schiltrons (defensive circles with pikes) possibly a 4th division

Scottish Order of Battle: 12 units

Commanding Officers:
Robert the Bruce, commanded rearguard at the entrance to New Park, Thomas Randolph, 1st Earl of Moray commanded the Scottish vanguard near church of St. Ninian, Edward the Bruce, led third division,
Sir James Douglas possibly led 4th division, Sir Robert Keith led cavalry

Right Flank	Left Flank	Center	Reserve
1 unit of light cavalry	3 units of infantry	3 units of infantry	3 units of infantry
3 units of infantry			

English Order of Battle: 18 units

Commanding Officers:
Edward II (Center &Vanguard), Earl of Gloucester, Gilbert de Clare and Humphrey de Bohun, Earlof Hereford (Left Flank), Robert Clifford (Right Flank)

Right Flank	Left Flank	Center
1 unit of heavy cavalry	1 unit of heavy cavalry	1 unit of heavy cavalry
4 units of infantry	4 units of infantry	4 units of infantry

Vanguard
3 units of missile infantry

Battlefield Conditions

Two Day Affair: A rare feat indeed during the Medieval Ages is conducting a two day battle. The forces above reflect the second day of the engagement.

Schiltrons: The Scottish schiltrons was essentially a formation of troops using long spears much like pikes to prevent successful cavalry charges. The schiltrons should receive a melee and possibly morale bonuses against cavalry making them difficult to fight against as well as break.

Armies meet at the river

The Commanders

Robert I (11 July 1274 – 7 June 1329), popularly known as Robert the Bruce, was King of Scots from 1306 until his death in 1329. Robert was one of the most famous warriors of his generation, and eventually led Scotland during the first of the Wars of Scottish Independence against England. He fought successfully during his reign to regain Scotland's place as an independent nation and is today remembered in Scotland as a national hero. Robert the Bruce died on 7 June 1329. His body is buried in Dunfermline Abbey, while his heart was interred in Melrose Abbey. Bruce's lieutenant and friend Sir James Douglas agreed to take the late King's embalmed heart on crusade to the Lord's Sepulchre in the Holy Land, but he reached only as far as Moorish Granada. Douglas was killed in battle during the siege of Teba while fulfilling his promise. His body and the casket containing the embalmed heart were found upon the field. They were both conveyed back to Scotland by Sir William Keith of Galston.

Edward II (25 April 1284 – 21 September 1327), also called Edward of Caernarfon, was King of England from 1307 until he was deposed in January 1327. The fourth son of Edward I, Edward became the heir to the throne following the death of his older brother Alphonso. Beginning in 1300, Edward accompanied his father on campaigns to pacify Scotland, and in 1306 he was knighted in a grand ceremony at Westminster Abbey. Edward succeeded to the throne in 1307, following his father's death. In 1308, he married Isabella of France, the daughter of the powerful King Philip IV, as part of a long-running effort to resolve the tensions between the English and French crowns. Unable to make progress in Scotland, Edward finally signed a truce with Robert. Opposition to the regime grew, and when Isabella was sent to France to negotiate a peace treaty in 1325, she turned against Edward and refused to return. Isabella allied herself with the exiled Roger Mortimer, and invaded England with a small army in 1326. Edward's regime collapsed and he fled into Wales, where he was captured in November. Edward was forced to relinquish his crown in January 1327 in favor of his son, Edward III, and he died in Berkeley Castle on 21 September, probably murdered on the orders of the new regime.

Robert I "the Bruce"

King Edward II

Battle of Morgarten

Date: 15 November 1315
Where: Morgarten Pass, Switzerland

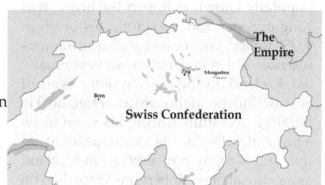

Opponents:
Old Swiss Confederacy – approximately 1,500 men
Duchy of Austria – approximately 8,000 men

Background:

At the end of the 13th century the Habsburg Empire was interested in acquiring the Gotthard Pass because it offered the shortest route to Italy, but the Swiss Confederates of Uri, Schwyz, and Unterwalden complicated the matter. Former Habsburg emperors granted the Swiss Confederacy local autonomy within the empire which was formalized in 1291 making the acquisition of the pass a political quagmire. The situation worsened in 1314 when Duke Louis IV of Bavaria and Frederick the Handsome, a Habsburg prince each vied for the position of Holy Roman Emperor. The Swiss Confederacy supported Louis IV because they were afraid the Habsburgs would annex their lands as they had attempted to do in the late 13th century. A negotiated position could not be reached and war eventually broke out between the Habsburgs and Swiss Confederacy.

Leopold, Frederick the Handsome's brother, assembled an army including a small contingent of knights to crush the Swiss rebellion. He planned a surprise attack coming in from the south of Lake Ägerisee through the Morgarten Pass. The Habsburg army's size is disputed but consisted of well-armed and well trained soldiers while the Confederate army was smaller, mainly militia, lacking the training and equipment that their opponents had.

Empire cavalry moving along the road

Swiss pikeman ambush the Empire troops

The Confederacy was given a warning of where and when the Habsburg army was marching which allowed the Swiss to prepare a roadblock and set an ambush between Lake Ägerisee and the Morgarten Pass. The area of the ambush was along a small path that went between a steep slope and a swamp so when the Confederates attacked the Austrians had very little room for escape. When the Habsburg army moved into the killzone the Confederates attacked from the slope with rocks, logs, arrows, and halberds. Unable to maneuver, the Austrian knights were slaughtered and the foot soldiers in the rear of the column retreated back to the city of Zug. The Swiss left little doubt to their position regarding the Hapsburg claims to the Swiss Passes by killing captured knights, rather than following the "civilized" rule of the day which allowed captured nobles to be ransomed. Any Austrian they caught fleeing or unable to escape was butchered.

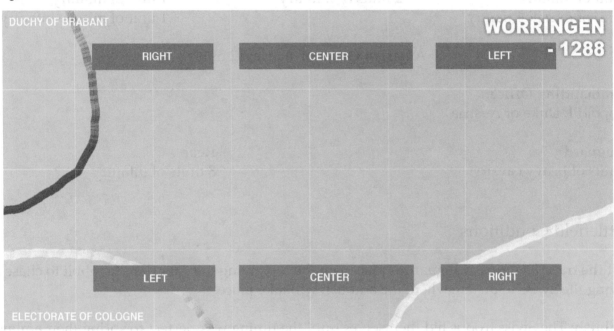

On the month following the battle in December 1315, the Confederates renewed their oath of allegiance to each other that was previously signed in 1291 giving the Swiss an opportunity to solidify their confederation. In March 1316, the Holy Roman Emperor Louis IV confirmed the rights and privileges of the Confederacy but the Swiss had to fend off Leopold and the Habsburgs once again. Neither side was ever able to gain an advantage over the other so by 1318 the Habsburgs and Swiss Confederacy signed a truce that would last for several years. The Confederacy continued to make alliances with Bern and Glarus in 1323 and over the next forty years cities such as Lucerne, Zug, and Zürich joined the Confederacy. The Confederacy enjoyed autonomy following this battle and did not fight with the Habsburgs again until 1386 at the Battle of Sempach.

Wargaming the Battle of Morgarten
Ratio- 1:2 (Swiss: Austrians)

Swiss Order of Battle: 6 units

Commanding Officer:
Werner Stauffacher

Slope ambush
1 unit of infantry
1 unit of missile infantry

Vanguard
2 units of infantry

Swamp ambush
1 unit of infantry
1 unit of missile infantry

Austrian Order of Battle: 12 units

Commanding Officer:
Leopold I, Duke of Austria

Vanguard
4 units of heavy cavalry

Rear
8 units of infantry

Battlefield Conditions

Bait the trap: The Swiss vanguard is placed on the top giving the Austrians 'a rabbit to chase' allowing the Swiss to dictate where the ambush will take place.

Ambush: The Swiss troops hid themselves until the timing was perfect to spring their ambush. The slope and swamp ambush units are held off table and in a single turn the units may be placed on the table springing their ambush. The rules governing this ambush will differ depending on the rulebook but it is recommended to keep the Swiss out of charge.

Narrow Pass: The Austrian formation is in a march-column and the pass only provides enough room for a few units to deploy. The game board should be played lengthwise and the sloping hill and swamp should reduce the ability for both forces to maneuver in the open.

Flanking units surprise the Imperials

The Commanders

Leopold I (4 August 1290 – 28 February 1326) Habsburg was Duke of Austria and Styria; which he co-ruled with his elder brother Frederick the Fair – from 1308 until his death. After the death of his eldest brother Duke Rudolph III in 1307 and the assassination of King Albert in 1308, Leopold became head of the Habsburg dynasty. Upon his ascension, he started a campaign of retaliation in the Swabian territories against his father's murderers. In 1311 he helped to suppress a Guelph revolt in Milan under Guido della Torre and laid siege to the city of Brescia. At the death of Emperor Henry, he supported his brother Frederick in the 1314 election as King of the Romans, but lost out to Louis IV of Wittelsbach. When Frederick and their younger brother Henry were captured at the Battle of Mühldorf in 1322, Leopold struggled for their release. He entered into negotiations with King Louis IV and even surrendered the Imperial Regalia he had kept at Kyburg castle. The parleys failed and Leopold continued to attack the Bavarian forces of Louis, who unsuccessfully laid siege to the Swabian town of Burgau in 1324. After the king had failed to reach the approval of his election by Pope John XXII and was even banned, he released Frederick in 1325. The captive however had to swear to his brother to acknowledge Louis as his suzerain, which Leopold refused. Frederick as a man of honor voluntarily returned to the Bavarian court, where he and Louis finally agreed upon a joint rule. Leopold died in Straßburg shortly afterwards, to the age of 35.

Werner Stauffacher was supposedly the name of the representative of the canton of Schwyz, one of the three founding cantons at the legendary Rütlischwur of 1291. Members of his family had held the office of Landammann of Schwyz during the 13th and 14th century.

An 18th century depiction of the three men of the Rutlischwur, including Werner Stauffacher (c)

Leopold I, Duke of Austria and Styria

Battle of Crécy

AKA: *Battle of Crecy, Battle of Cressy*
Date: 26 August 1346
Where: Crécy-en-Ponthieu, Somme, France

Opponents:
Kingdom of England and Holy Roman Empire
                    – approximately 15,000 men
Kingdom of France and Genoese with mercenaries
(Kingdom of Navarre, Kingdom of Bohemia,
Kingdom of Majorca) – approximately 30,000 men

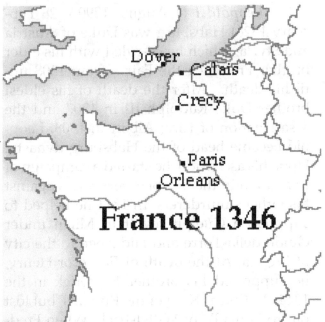

France 1346

Background:

During the Hundred Years' War King Edward III of England planned an invasion of France through Flanders but the attack failed because of financial difficulties and unstable alliances. Six more years passed before Edward could properly plan the next invasion but this time the English army landed in Normandy winning the battles of Caen and Blanchetaque on 26 July and 24 August respectively. The French planned to trap and capture the English army between the Seine and Somme rivers but it failed and the English escaped setting up one of the major conflicts of the war.

Upon landing in France the English army marched several miles each day and only met with minor French resistance. King Edward III arrived at the forest of Crécy and deployed on a small hill with the town of Wadicourt protecting their left flank and the River Maye securing their right flank. The English force marched over 300 miles and arrived first giving them a day to rest before the French arrived. Unfortunately for the French, the army marched straight into battle hampering their abilities to fight effectively.

King Edward III divided his force into three divisions with the vanguard led by Edward, Prince of Wales; the central division controlled by the king himself and the rearguard under the generalship of William de Bohun, Earl of Northampton. The entire English force consisted of around 2,700-2,800 men-at-arms including the English king, nobles with their retinues and other low ranking knights. Along with the men-at-arms, the English army also had approximately 11,000-13,000 other troops consisting of

Men-at-Arms from the Crecy period (courtesy Fire Forge Games)

2,300 Welsh spearman, 7,000 Welsh and English foot archers, and 3,250 mounted archers and light cavalry. The records of the French army have been lost to history but the estimates have the French outnumbering their English counter parts with approximately 12,000 mounted men-at-arms, perhaps as many as 6,000 Genoese crossbowmen, and an undetermined amount of common infantry.

King Edward III deployed his army in a defensive formation strung along a hill and he ordered all of his soldiers to fight on foot. The long-bowmen were organized into a 'V-formation' along the crest of the hill and while waiting for the French to arrive the English dug ditches and built pits and caltrops to defend against any cavalry charges. The men-at-arms fighting alongside the archers kept the English army together and not only prevented a premature cavalry charge but kept the men-at-arms fighting under the protection of their archers. The presence of the knights fighting on foot also bolstered the morale of the archers and kept keeping them in line for a longer period of time.

Without resting, the French army marched onto the battlefield and deployed their Genoese crossbowmen in the front line supported by French cavalry. The crossbowmen left their pavises on the baggage carts denying their only protection against English arrows. Both forces began to exchange missile fire but the range and increased rate of the fire of the English longbow compared to the crossbows forced the Genoese to retreat only to be mercilessly butchered by the frustrated French nobles. With the covering fire of the crossbowman gone, the mounted knights pushed forward and began their charge only to be bogged down by the man-made obstacles and withering fire of the longbows. Wave upon wave of French cavalry hit the English lines and each successive charge was repulsed. The battle raged on until nightfall and when Philip was wounded a general retreat was ordered.

The English victory at Crécy established the dominance of the longbow as a potent weapon against heavily armored knights and established a British presence in France that lasted until the end of the war. The Black Prince 'earned his spurs' during the battle proving to his father that he was a skilled fighter and became the king's best field commander.

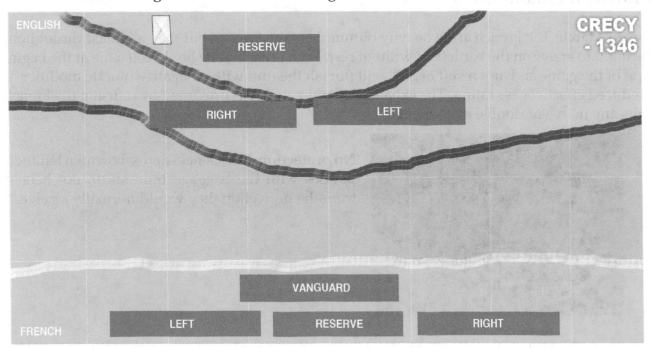

Wargaming the Battle of Crécy
Ratio- 1:2 (English: French)

English Order of Battle: 9 units

Commanding Officers:

Edward III of England (Reserve); Edward, the Black Prince (Right Flank); William De Bohun, the 1st Earl of Northampton (Left Flank)

Right Flank	Left Flank	Reserve
2 units of missile infantry	2 units of missile infantry	2 units of heavy cavalry
1 unit of infantry (Welsh)	1 unit of infantry (Welsh)	1 unit of light cavalry

French Order of Battle: 18 units

Commanding Officers:

Philip VI of France (Reserve), John of Bohemia (Vanguard), Count of Blois (Right Flank) Duke of Lorraine (Left Flank)

Right Flank	Left Flank	Vanguard
4 units of heavy cavalry	3 units of heavy cavalry	3 units of missile infantry (Genoese)

Reserve

8 units of infantry

Battlefield Conditions

Forced March: The French army heavily outnumbers the English but they marched throughout the night to arrive on the battlefield without rest. Each French unit should roll a die at the beginning of the game and any result of a '1' will punish the unit with a negative morale modifier or a reduced effectiveness rating. The exhaustion could also be represented by refusing the French units any march or double movements.

No protection: The Genoese crossbowmen left their pavises with the baggage train so do not benefit from the protection they would normally receive.

English longbowmen

The Commanders

Edward III (13 November 1312 – 21 June 1377) was King of England from 25 January 1327 until his death; he is noted for his military success and for restoring royal authority after the disastrous reign of his father, Edward II. Edward III transformed the Kingdom of England into one of the most formidable military powers in Europe. His long reign of fifty years was the second longest in medieval England and saw vital developments in legislation and government — in particular the evolution of the English parliament — as well as the ravages of the Black Death. After a successful campaign in Scotland he declared himself rightful heir to the French throne in 1337 but his claim was denied due to the Salic law. This started what would become known as the Hundred Years' War. Following some initial setbacks the war went exceptionally well for England; victories at Crécy and Poitiers led to the highly favorable Treaty of Brétigny. Edward's later years, however, were marked by international failure and domestic strife, largely as a result of his inactivity and poor health.

Philip VI (French: Philippe VI) (1293 – 22 August 1350) earned the nickname, "the Fortunate" and was the first King of France from the House of Valois. He reigned from 1328 until his death. Philip's reign was dominated by the consequences of a succession dispute. When King Charles IV the Fair died without a male heir in 1328, the nearest male relative was his nephew Edward III of England, who inherited his claim through his mother Isabella of France, the sister of the dead king. It was held in France, however, that Edward was ineligible to inherit the French throne through the female line according to the ancient Salic Law. At first, Edward seemed to accept Philip's accession as the nearest male relative of Charles IV descended through the male line, however he pressed his claim to the throne of France after a series of disagreements with Philip. The result was the beginning of the Hundred Years' War in 1337. After initial successes at sea, Philip's navy was annihilated at the Battle of Sluys in 1340, ensuring that the war would occur on the continent. The English took another decisive advantage at the Battle of Crécy (1346), while the Black Death struck France, further destabilizing the country. Philip VI died in 1350 and was succeeded by his son John II the Good.

Effigy of Edward III from his tomb in Westminster

Philip VI, "the Fortunate" of France

Battle of Poitiers

Date: 19 September 1356
Where: Poitiers, France

Opponents:
England and Gascony – approximately 6,000 men
France – approximately 20,000 men

Background:

England and France were heavily embroiled in war for almost 20 years and on 8 August 1356 Edward, Prince of Wales (Black Prince) started a scorched earth campaign known as achevauchée. The English army started in Aquitaine and ravaged the countryside burning settlements and living off the land until they arrived at the Loire River near Tours. The torrential downpour of rain prevented Edward from taking the castle or burning the settlement and this gave John II, King of France, time to intercept the English. John II was in the process of besieging Breteuil in Normandy but abandoned his campaign to catch up with Edward. Prior to the battle of Poitiers nobles from both England and France, including King John II, met hoping to avoid bloodshed but the results of the meeting was inconclusive and conflict was imminent.

The two armies deployed for battle and the English decided to remove their baggage train which prompted the French to think they were withdrawing and it provoked a hasty charge towards the English archers. Volleys of arrows rained upon Clermont's French cavalry and the horses were specifically targeted to break up the cohesion of the charge. The casualties were severe and the French vanguard was forced to withdraw. The Dauphin pressed the attack against Salisbury's troops but disorder and confusion was created when Clermont's force retreated through his soldiers. The Dauphin was also forced to withdraw unable to breakthrough the strong English defensive formation

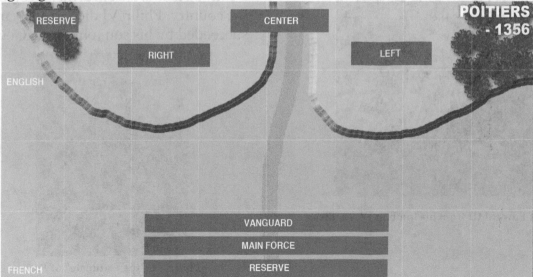

English archers behind prepared positions

After two hours of fighting and a failed cavalry assault, the Dauphin sent his infantry forward resulting in heavy fighting which forced his troops to withdraw. The second infantry wave was led by Orléans but seeing that the Dauphin's men had withdrawn and were not fighting they retreated in panic. The only remaining fighting force was led by King John II and though the English were running low on arrows they were still a huge threat. The English archers consolidated with the other infantry and many of them mounted horses creating improvised cavalry.

King John and his eldest son Philip led their troops into the frenetic battle line, but Edward had a mobile reserve hiding in the woods. The English reserve led by Jean deGrailly the Captal de Buch, emerged at the rear of the French line and caused chaos among the French soldiers forcing many to flee. King John and his entourage fought valiantly but inevitably they were captured. The English ended up capturing several French nobles and the victory created instability all over France.

The battle of Poitiers was the second of the three great English victories during the Hundred Years' War with the third triumph not to take place for almost 60 years.

Wargaming the Battle ofPoitiers
Ratio- 1:3 (English: French)

English Order of Battle: 6 units

Commanding Officers:
Edward, the Black Prince of Wales (Center),Earl of Warwick (Left Flank),Earl of Salisbury (Right Flank), Jean de Grailly, Captal de Buch (Reserve)

Right Flank
1 unit of missile infantry

Left Flank
1 unit of missile infantry

Center
1 unit of infantry
2 units of heavy cavalry

Reserve
1 unit of heavy cavalry

Genovese crossbowman in the pay of the French

French Order of Battle: 18 units

Commanding Officers:
John II and Philip of France (Reserve), Baron Clermont (Vanguard); Dauphin Charles, Duke of Orleans (MainForce)

Main Force
2 units of missile infantry
6 units of infantry

Vanguard
4 units of heavy cavalry

Reserve
2 units of missile infantry
4 units of infantry

Battlefield Conditions

Graily's reserve: Jean de Graily was ordered to hide a unit of elite heavy cavalry in the woods and wait for the opportune time to strike. His unit is held in reserve and brought in at the beginning of any turn after the first turn.

The battle of Poitiers from a contemporary picture

The battle of Poitiers from a series by Froissart showing the oriflamme in the French ranks

The Commanders

Edward of Woodstock (15 June 1330 – 8 June 1376), called the Black Prince, was the eldest son of King Edward III, and the father of King Richard II of England. He was the first Duke of Cornwall (from 1337), the Prince of Wales (from 1343) and the Prince of Aquitaine (1362–72). He was an exceptional military leader, and his victories over the French at the Battles of Crécy and Poitiers made him very popular during his lifetime. In 1348 he became the first Knight of the Garter, of whose order he was one of the founders. Edward died one year before his father, becoming the first English Prince of Wales not to become King of England.

John II (26 April 1319 – 8 April 1364), or Jean II, also called John the Good was a monarch of the House of Valois who ruled as King of France from 1350 until his death. John II came to power facing several disasters: the Black Death, which caused the death of nearly half of its population; popular revolts known as Jacqueries; free companies of routiers who plundered the country; and English aggression that resulted in disastrous military losses, including the Battle of Poitiers of 1356, in which John was captured. While John was a prisoner in London, his son Charles became regent. To liberate his father, he concluded the Treaty of Brétigny (1360), which ceded a large amount of territory as well as a large ransom. John was exchanged for other hostages, including his son Louis, but when Louis escaped from captivity, he voluntarily returned to England, dying there in 1364. He was succeeded by his son Charles V.

The effigy of the Black Prince from his tomb

John II, "the Good", of France

Battle of Nájera

Date: 3 April 1367
Where: Nájera, Spain

Opponents:

Crown of Castile, Kingdom of England, Duchy of Aquitaine, Kingdom of Mallorca and Gascony
　　　　　　　　–approximately 28,000 men

Crown of Castile, Kingdom of France
　　　　　　　　– approximately 60,000 men

Background:

　　　　The realm of Castile became a flashpoint for conflict during the 1360s when two brothers went to war over the throne. Pedro the Cruel, was the reigning King of Castile but his nobles despised him. Peter was considered a tyrant and he over-extended his authority when he went to war with Aragon. At that time, his brother, Henry of Trastámara was living in France where he assembled an army and invaded Castile. He forced Peter to flee to Bayonne, an English held city in Gascony, and Henry became the King of Castile, León, Toledo, and Seville. Henry quickly gained the favor of the Castilian nobles as well as France, Aragon, and the Papacy. During Pedro's exile he petitioned the Black Prince, Edward, for aid and in exchange for military intervention he would reward Edward with lands and title in Castile. The Black Prince assembled an English army and with Pedro at his side they returned to Castile.

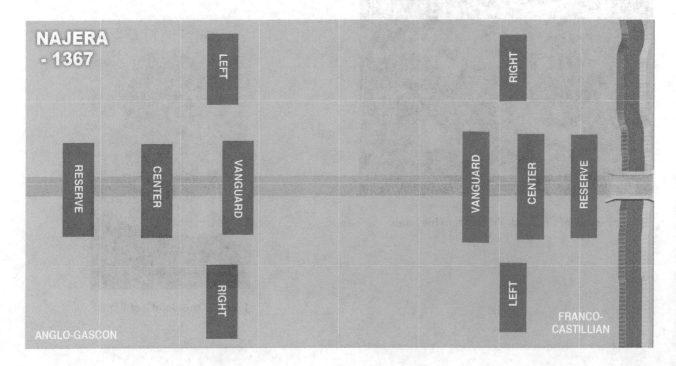

An army of around 28,000 Anglo-Gascon men marched from Aquitaine and quickly took control of the fortified village of Navarrete. They continued their march towards Nájera to meet up with Henry's Franco-Castilian army numbering close to 60,000 soldiers. The two armies faced each other in a pitched battle that began with a duel between the English long-bowmen and French archers. John of Gaunt, the Duke of Lancaster, along with the free companies, positioned themselves in the vanguard and charged into the French mercenaries led by Du Guesclin and Amoul D'Audrehem.

The French cavalry received withering fire from the English long-bowmen and they retired early in the battle. Their departure left Henry's battle (division) exposed and the English rearguard moved in to attack. The Franco-Castilian army began to disintegrate and retreated back to the Najerilla River. The victory restored Pedro to the Castilian throne but overall the results of the battle had no long-term significance.

Wargaming the Battle of Nájera
Ratio- 1:2 (Anglo-Gascon: Franco-Castilian)

Anglo-Gascon Order of Battle: 15 units

Commanding Officers:
Edward, the Black Prince of Wales (Center), John of Gaunt, Duke of Lancaster (Vanguard), Percy (Right Flank), De Buch (Left Flank), Count of Armagnac and King of Majorca (Reserve)

Right Flank
1 unit of missile infantry
1 unit of infantry

Left Flank
1 unit of missile infantry
1 unit of infantry

Center
1 unit of missile infantry
3 units of infantry

Vanguard
2 units of missile infantry
2 units of infantry

Reserve
1 unit of missile infantry
2 units of infantry

The Anglo-Gascon line attacks

Franco-Castilian Order of Battle: 30 units

Commanding Officers:
Henry II of Castile (Center), Bertrand du Guesclin & Amoul D'Audrehem (Vanguard), Don Tello (Left Flank), Carillo de Quintana (Right Flank)

Right Flank	**Left Flank**	**Center**
1 unit of missile infantry	1 unit of missile infantry	Units of heavy cavalry
1 unit of heavy cavalry	1 unit of heavy cavalry	

Vanguard	**Reserve**
3 units of missile infantry	18 units of infantry (Spanish)
3 units of infantry	

Battlefield Conditions

French Arrogance: The French aristocracy is only interested in victories that are won from the sweat of French soldiers. The Spanish reserve is held off table and only comes into play indire need. Once the French side has lost at least 4 units then the Spanish will be called into play.

Image of Najera by Froissart

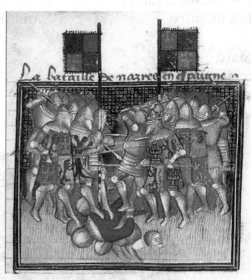

Contemporary drawing of the battle of Najera

The Commanders

Pedro the Cruel (30 August 1334 – 23 March 1369), also known as the Just, was the king of Castile and León from 1350 to 1369. He was the son of Alfonso XI of Castile and the last ruler of the main branch of the House of Ivrea. In the summer of 1366, Peter took refuge with Edward, the Black Prince, who restored him to his throne in the following year after the Battle of Nájera. He fell out quickly with his allies however, because of he did not keep his pledges to rewarding his success and double dealing.

He was eventually deposed by Henry of Trastámara in 1369 and assassinated with the help of Bertrand du Guesclin, who Pedro tried to entice to turn on Henry.

Pedro, "the Cruel" or "the Just" depending which side you were on

Henry II (13 January 1334 – 29 May 1379) was the first King of Castile and León from the House of Trastámara. He became king in 1369 by defeating his half-brother, King Peter, after numerous rebellions and battles. As king he was involved in the Ferdinand Wars and the Hundred Years' War. Henry was the fourth of ten illegitimate children of King Alfonso XI of Castile and Eleanor de Guzmán, a great-granddaughter of Alfonso IX of León. He was born a twin to Fadrique Alfonso, Lord of Haro, and was the first boy born to the couple that survived to adulthood. At birth, he was adopted by Rodrigo Álvarez de las Asturias. Rodrigo died the following year and Henry inherited his lordship of Noreña. His father later made him Count of Trastámara and lord over Lemos and Sarria in Galicia, and the towns of Cabrera and Ribera, which constituted a large and important heritage in the northeast of the peninsula. It made him the head of the new Trastámara dynasty, arising from the main branch of Burgundy-Ivrea. While Alfonso XI lived, his lover Eleanor gave a great many titles and privileges to their sons. This caused discontent among many of the noblemen and in particular the queen, Maria of Portugal, and her son, Pedro. When Alfonso XI died unexpectedly from a fever in 1350, Eleanor, her sons and their supporters were pushed aside and scattered. Eventually Pedro picked apart Eleanor and her sons until Henry found support from Aragon and France. Eventually, he killed Pedro and assumed the crown.

Henry II of Castile

Battle of Aljubarrota

Date: 14 August 1385
Where: Aljubarrota, Portugal

Opponents:
Kingdom of Portugal and Kingdom of England
            – approximately 6,500 men

Crown of Castile, Kingdom of France and Aragonese
            – approximately 31,000 men

Background:

      The crisis permiating the 14th century extended to the Iberian Peninsula in the Kingdom of Portugal. In October 1383, King Ferdinand I died with no apparent heir to the throne. In April 1383, before Ferdinand's death a treaty was signed acknowledging the marriage between Lenor Telles de Meneses, Princess Beatrice of Portugal, and Juan I, King of Castile. Unfortunately, the Portuguese nobility and powerful merchants were outraged by this decision and the disagreement left the throne vacant for two years.

      In December 1383, John, the Grand Master of the Aviz Order, murdered Count Andeiro prompting the merchants to declare him 'rector and defender of the realm'. King Juan was reluctant to give up his right to the Portuguese throne and in April 1384 a Castilian punitive expedition was launched but defeated at the Battle of Atoleiros. John of Aviz opened intense political and diplomatic negotiations to ensure the safety of Portugal and maintain his dominance over the realm. Richard II of England supported John and on 6 April 1385, on the anniversary of the victory at the battle of Atoleiros, John of Aviz was declared King John I of Portugal. His first order was to annex cities under his control but the military commanders in cities such as Caminha, Braga, and Guimarães remained loyal to Princess Beatrice.

      Infuriated by these actions Juan I ordered an invasion of Portugal by splitting his attack into two prongs. The smaller of the two Castilian forces sacked and burned cities, but was eventually defeated by a quickly assembled Portuguese force lead by the local nobles at the Battle of Trancoso. When word reached John I, he assembled his army to meet the Castilians before they could reach Lisbon. Around 100 English long-bowmen arrived on Easter to join the Portuguese army honoring the Anglo-Portuguese Treaty of 1373, the oldest active treaty current in the world today. The combined forces defending Portugal under the banner of John I set out to intercept the Castilians near the town of Leiria taking up positions on the northern slope of a hill.

      The vanguard of the Castilian army ar-

The allied Portugese meet the French

rived around lunch time and seeing the strong defenses of the Portuguese they decided to circumnavigate the hill to engage the Portuguese in a more favorable position. The Portuguese army reversed its position and marched to the southsideof the hill arriving in the early afternoon to wait for the reappearance of the Castilian army.

The Portuguese commander Nuno Álvares Pereira ordered the construction of a network of ditches, trenches and caltrops to protect the army's rear and use as a defensive position if the battle shifted. At six o'clock the Castilian army arrayed itself at the bottom of the hill. The army was tired from the day's march in the hot August sun but there was no time to rest. The Castilian army contained allied French heavy cavalry and they began the arduous journey up the hill towards the Portuguese lines. The cavalry was quickly disorganized by the defending archers, crossbowmen, and vast array of cavalry pits as they took heavy losses without having any effect against their enemy. The main Castilian force moved up the hill but was too far behind the French cavalry to offer any assistance. The Castilian commanders had to squeeze their troops together in order to fit between the two creeks that protected the Portuguese flanks and in the process disorganized themselves.

Meanwhile, John relieved his archers and crossbowmen so the reserve forces could advance to engage in melee. The two lines crashed together and both forces sustained heavy casualties as the mounted heavy knights on the wings of the Castilian army punished both flanks. The Portuguese lines held and one hour into the battle the Castilian position became untenable. The royal standard bearer of Castile fell and the army thought that the loss of their banner meant the death of their king so the already exhausted and demoralized troops of the Castilian army fled in panic.

Throughout the evening and into the next day over 5,000 Castilian soldiers were killed in the Portuguese countryside as they tried to escape. John I finally offered the surviving soldiers amnesty and free transit home as Castile went into mourning for almost two years. The victory at Aljubarrota secured John of Aviz's ascendency to the Portuguese throne although it was not until 1411 with the signature of the Treat of Ayllón that Castile would recognize him as king.

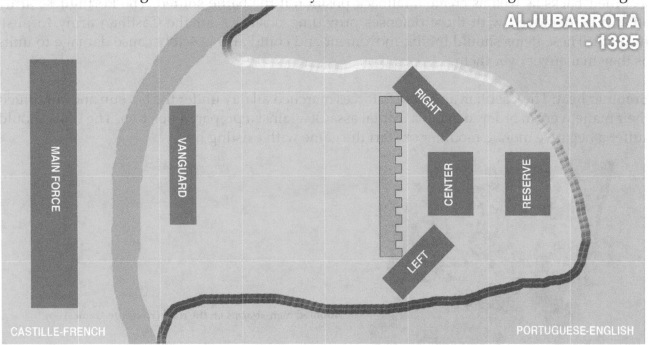

Wargaming the Battle of Aljubarrota
Ratio- 1:5 (Portuguese/English: Castilan/French)

Portuguese and English Order of Battle: 6 units

Commanding Officers:
John I of Portugal (Reserve), Nuno Álvares Pereira

Right Flank
1 unit of heavy cavalry
(Ala de Madressilva – Honeysuckle Flank)

Left Flank
1 unit of heavy cavalry)
(Ala dos Namorados–Sweethearts Flank)

Center
1 unit of missile infantry
1 unit of infantry

Reserve
2 units of infantry

Castile & French Order of Battle: 30 units

Commanding Officers:
John I of Castile, Nuno Álvares Pereira

Vanguard
8 units of heavy cavalry

Main Force
15 units of infantry
7 units of missile infantry

Battlefield Conditions

Defenses: Pereira had a series of pits, trenches and caltrops built in the rear of the army to protect their backs as well as create a fallback position if the battle shifted. The Portuguese army should be deployed with these defenses providing obstacles for the Castilian army to push through. These items should inhibit movement and could also possibly cause damage to units as they maneuver over them.

Summer heat: The Castilian and French forces marched all day under the hot sun and continued their maneuvers in order to avoid a frontal assault against a prepared position. The units should suffer a negative morale modifier or start the game with existing hits.

Mounted men-at-arms on the road (Fireforge Games)

The Commanders

John I (11 April 1358 – 14 August 1433) was King of Portugal and the Algarve in 1385–1433. He was called the Good (sometimes the Great) or Happy Memory, more rarely and outside Portugal, in Spain, the Bastard, and was the first to use the title Lord of Ceuta. He preserved the kingdom's independence from Castile. After the death of John I of Castile in 1390, John I of Portugal pursued the economic development of the country. The only significant military action was the siege and conquest of the city of Ceuta in 1415.

Juan I (24 August 1358 – 9 October 1390) was King of the Crown of Castile from 1379 until 1390. He was the son of Henry II. He was the last Spanish monarch to receive a formal coronation in Portugal. King John of Castile invaded Portugal in the end of December 1383, to enforce his claim to be king. The consequent war ended in 1385, with the defeat of Castile in the Battle of Aljubarrota. In the aftermath of this battle, John of Aviz became the uncontested King of Portugal. John of Castile and Beatrice no longer had a tenable claim to the throne of Portugal, but during the lifetime of John I of Castile, they continued to call themselves king and queen of Portugal.

John I, "the Good", King of Portugal and Algarve

Juan I, King of Castile

Battle of Kosovo

AKA: *Battle of Kosovo Field, Battle of Blackbird's Field*
Date: 15 June 1389
Where: Kosovo field, Moravian Serbia

Opponents:
Ottoman Empire – approximately 30,000 men
Serbian Principality and Kingdom of Bosnia
          – approximately 20,000 men

Background:

Centralized Serbian control over its principalities was in steady decline during the late 14th century and was commonly referred to as the "fall of the Serbian Empire". Emperor Stefan Uroš Valso, known as Uroš the Weak, was not able to maintain the empire that he inherited from his father nor was he capable of fending off foreign invaders and limiting the independence of the nobles. Uroš V died on 4 December 1371 without any children and the Battle of Maritsa earlier in the year killed many of the nobles that were capable of sitting on the throne. Prince Lazar, ruler of Moravian Serbia, predicted the Ottoman threat and began diplomatic and military preparations for the war against theTurks.

The Ottomans had suffered defeats at Pločnik in 1386 and again at Bileća in 1388 so Murad I,the reigning sultan, decided to redeploy his troops in the spring of 1388 and march them to Kosovo where he could attack Lazar's or Vuk Branković's territory. His army moved through the towns of Kumanovo, Preševo, Gnjilane and arrived in Pristina on 14 June 1389. In the meantime, Lazar and his forces were gathering in Niš when he received word that Murad moved to Velbužd. Lazar assembled his army and marched to Kosovo where he could block all of the possible routes that Murad could utilize.

The Turks marched onto Kosovo Field with Murad leading the center of his army along

Attack on the Serbian line

with his sons Bayezid and Yakub who commanded the right and left flanks respectfully. Murad deployed approximately 1,000 archers in front of the left and right wings with additional Azap (litteraly "the bachelors", Ottoman Light Infantry) and Akıncı (Ottoman Light cavalry) in support. At the center of the Ottoman army were Janissaries and Murad's cavalry guard behind them. The Serbian force was led by Lazar in the center, Vuk Branković on the right flank, Vlatko Vuković on the left, and an infantry reserve in the rear.

Ottoman archers started the battle shooting full volleys into the Serbian cavalry but their charge pushed through, hitting along the entire Turkish line. The V-shaped cavalry formations broke through on the Ottoman left wing but were rebuffed in the center and on the right flank. The Serbs pressed the advantage after the initial charge and Yakub Celebi's Turkish troops were being decimated until Ottoman light cavalry and light infantry counter-attacked.

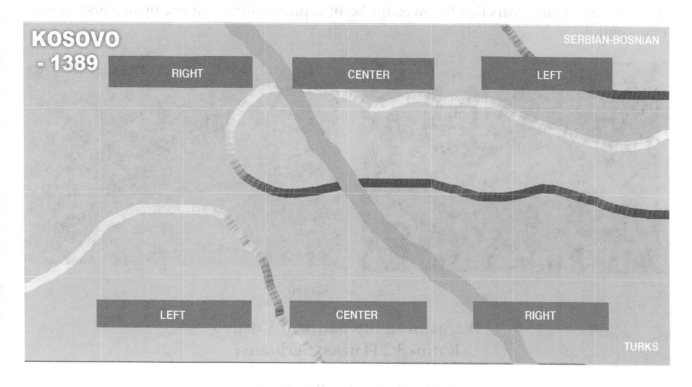

The Serbians in the center pushed the Turks back but Vlatko was unable to break Bayezid's wing. Vlatko's and Bayezid's forces suffered enormous casualties while both sides were attempting to gain the upper hand. Later in the conflict, Bayezid conducted a counter-attack pushing the Serbian infantry off the field of battle. Vlatko pinched his forces towards the center of battlefield to compensate for the heavy losses as the Ottoman army continued to press the advantage. Surveying the carnage and learning of Lazar's capture, Vuk Branković realized the battle was lost and began to withdraw his troops trying to save as many lives as possible.

At some point during the battle the Ottoman sultan, Murad, was killed and his death is surrounded by mystery. There are several theories including that a Serbian knight, Mi-

Turkish cavalry attacks the Serbian line

loš Obilić, pretended to desert to the Turks so he could confront Murad and kill him. When Bayezid was informed of his father's death he sent false information to his brother Yakub and had him strangled leaving him the sole heir to the Ottoman Empire.

Lazar and Murad lost their lives during the battle and as a result both forces retreated from the field battered and bloodied. The Serbians were unable to recover from the losses in the battle and in the years that followed the Serbian principalities fell one by one under Ottoman control.

Attack on the wagon forts

Wargaming the Battle of Kosovo
Ratio- 3:2 (Turks: Serbians)

Turks Order of Battle: 30 units

Commanding Officers:
Sultan Murad (Center), Bayezid (Right Flank), Yakub Celebi (Left Flank)

Right Flank
3 units of missile infantry (azaps)
4 units of infantry (akıncıs)
3 units of heavy cavalry (sipahis)
2 units of infantry (vassal troops)

Left Flank
3 units of missile infantry (azaps)
4 units of infantry (akıncıs)
3 units of heavy cavalry (sipahis)
2 units of infantry (vassal troops)

Center
2 units of infantry (Janissaries)
2 units of heavy cavalry (cavalry guard)
2 units of infantry (vassal troops)
2 units of artillery

Serbian and Bosnian Order of Battle: 20 units

Commanding Officers:
Prince Lazar (Center), Vuk Branković (Right Flank), Vlatko Vuković (Left Flank)

Right Flank
2 units of missile infantry
3 units of heavy cavalry
1 unit of infantry

Left Flank
2 units of missile infantry
3 units of cavalry
1 unit of infantry

Center
2 units of missile infantry
3 units of cavalry
2 units of infantry
2 units of artillery

Battlefield Conditions

Hidden ditches: The Turks dug camouflaged ditches that were lined with stakes just behind the archers. The positions of the ditches are placed once the archers have been deployed so the positions will change from battle to battle. These obstacles will slow down a units advance as well as cause damage to it. The ditches could cause negative morale modifiers, hits to the unit moving through them or some type of disorder.

Ottomans reinforce their defensive lines

The Commanders

Murad I (29 June 1326 – 15 June 1389) was the sultan of the Ottoman Empire from 1362 to 1389. He was a son of Orhan and the Valide Sultan Nilüfer Hatun. Murad I conquered Adrianople, renamed it to Edirne and in 1363 made it the new capital of Ottoman Empire. Then he further expanded the Ottoman realm in Southeast Europe by bringing most of the Balkans under Ottoman rule, and forced the princes of northern Serbia and Bulgaria as well as the Byzantine emperor John V Palaiologos to pay him tribute. Murad I administratively divided his empire into the two provinces of Anatolia (Asia Minor) and Rumelia (the Balkans). He was killed at Kosovo, allegedly by Miloš Obilić, who managed to get through the Ottoman army and kill Murad I together with his son Yakub. Sultan Murad's internal organs were buried in Kosovo field and remains to this day on a corner of the battlefield in a location called Meshed-i Hudavendigar.

Prince Lazar Hrebeljanović (ca. 1329 – 15 June 1389) was a medieval Serbian ruler, who created the largest and most powerful state on the territory of the disintegrated Serbian Empire. Lazar's state, known in historiography as Moravian Serbia, comprised Great Morava, West Morava, and South Morava Rivers. Lazar ruled it from 1373 until his death in 1389. Lazar's political program was the reunification of the disintegrated Serbian state under him as the direct successor of the Nemanjić dynasty, which ended in 1371. In the Battle of Kosovo fought on 15 June 1389, Lazar led the army which confronted a massive invading army of the Ottoman Empire commanded by Sultan Murad I. Both Prince Lazar and Sultan Murad lost their lives in the battle. Although the battle was tactically inconclusive, the mutual heavy losses were devastating only for the Serbs. Lazar's widow, Milica, who ruled as regent for her minor son Stefan Lazarević, Lazar's successor, accepted Ottoman suzerainty in the summer of 1390.

Murad I

Prince Lazar

Battle of Nicopolis

Date: 25 September 1396
Where: Nicopolis, Bulgaria

Opponents:

Ottoman Empire and Moravian Serbia
                    – approximately 15,000 men

Holy Roman Empire, Kingdom of France, Kingdom of Hungary, Wallachia, Knights Hospitaller, Republic of Venice, Republic of Genoa, Second Bulgarian Empire – approximately 16,000 men

Balkans 1396

Background:

After the Battle of Kosovo in 1389, the Ottomans had conquered most of the Balkans and in 1393 the Bulgarian Tsar Ivan Shishman lost Nicopolis to the Turks. As the Crusade raged across Europe to reconquer lost lands, the focus of the religious war shifted slowly towards the Kingdom of Hungary. Philip II, Duke of Burgundy, sponsored a crusade to defend the Christian lands from the Turks and protect the Kingdom of Hungary. Burgundy took 120,000 livres from Flanders and with enough money he began his preparations for the crusade. In January 1395 Philip II sent word to Sigismund, King of Hungary, that if he sent an official request to the King of France to aid the crusade he would accept the offer. In August, Sigismund sent a delegation of four knights and a bishop to Paris and convinced Charles VI that a crusade in Hungary to defend Europe was in his best interests. Eventually, a grand alliance of Christians from all over Europe was created to include France, Hungry, the Bulgarian Empire, Wallachia, Venice, Genoa, the Rhineland, Bavaria, Saxony, Poland, Bohemia, Navarre, and Spain.

Philip of Burgundy originally intended on leading the great Crusade into Hungry along with John of Gaunt and Louis of Orleans but all three remained behind to monitor the peace negotiations between England and France. Philip maintained financial responsibility for the Chris-

tian army and sent his eldest son, John de Nevers, to take nominal command of the force. John was only 24-years-old and lacked the experience to run such a large force so Philip summoned Enguerrand VII, Lord of Coucy, a very experienced warrior, to act as chief counselor to John.

The army marched out of Dijon on 30 April 1396 and moved through Bavaria to the Danube where they would join with Sigismund and take the river to Buda. The accumulation of all of the soldiers and commanders took some time but by July everyone was assembled in Buda. With everyone present Philibert de Naillac, Master of the Knights Hospitaller, began coordinating the

Christian forces move forward

Ottoman cavalry attacks the Christian line

strategy of the attack. Although the council of war had serious disagreements regarding the plan of attack, the army ended up marching down the left bank of the Danube while part of the Hungarian army split off to recruit more soldiers from Transylvania and Wallachia. The Christian army moved into Turkish held Bulgaria and quickly recaptured Vidin before moving onto Oryahovo. The French troops were frustrated by the lack of action so they performed a force march to arrive at Oryahovo before anyone else and prevented the Turks from destroying the bridge across the moat. The rest of the army arrived in the evening forcing the Turks back within the safety of the fortress walls, but the following morning the Ottoman's surrendered.

A garrison was left behind at Oryahovo and the rest of the army continued on to Nicopolis sacking a few forts and settlements along the way but ignored a citadel which allowed Turkish messengers to escape and warn Bayezid of the imminent Christian arrival. On 12 September the crusaders moved within sight of the Nicopolis fortress on the heights of its limestone cliff. The fortress was actually two fortified towns with one positioned at the foot of the cliff and the other located on the cliff itself. The fortress was in a naturally defensive position which controlled the lower Danube and anyone wishing to communicate inland. The fortress was well-defended and aptly supplied with only a small road which hugged the cliff and the river allowing access to the interior. The Turkish governor, Doğan Bey, was prepared to hold out against a long siege but realized that he would need the army under Sultan Bayezid's banner to relieve his defense. The crusaders surrounded the fortress, set up siege positions to prevent anyone from exiting, and the established a naval blockade to starve out the Turks.

Two weeks passed and the crusading force distracted themselves with games and insulting

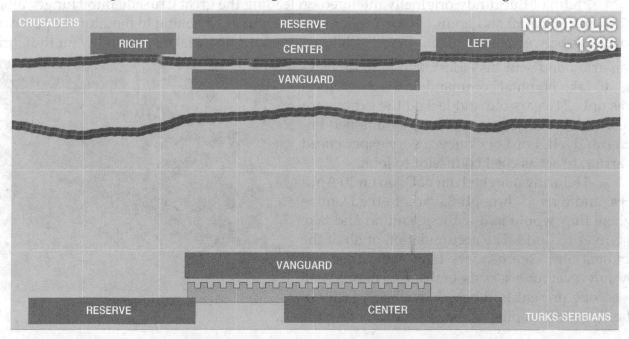

Turkish cavalry attack the christian left

the enemy but over time they neglected to post sentries. Meanwhile, Bayezid was on a force march to engage the Christians and during his trek he picked up his ally, Stefan Lazarević of Serbia. Coucy began to concern himself about scouting the area for the Turks and he set out with 500 knights and 500 mounted archers to find the enemy. The scouting party found the Turks marching through a pass and set up an ambush killing as many Turks as possible before returning to camp. Upon their return, the crusaders were shaken awake with excitement for the pending engagement.

Sigismund assembled a war council on 24 September and it was agreed to assign Mircea of Wallachia, whose troops had experience fighting the Turks, to engage the leading elements of the Ottoman army because Sigismund did not want to exhaust his knights on masses of militia. The vanguard of the Ottoman army was typically poorly armed militia which would be used to wear down the opponent before the attack of their higher quality troops. The French forces would follow up on the initial attack with the remaining forces providing support and preventing anyTurkish cavalry from flanking.

At dawn on the 25th and the Christian forces began to arrange themselves on the battlefield under the banners of their leaders. Sigismund sent his Grand Master to Nevers to inform him that they spotted the vanguard of the Turkish army and requested to hold the attack for two hours giving scouts enough time to reconnoiter the enemy's force. After a fierce dispute regarding the advance of the army Jean I, Count of Nevers decided to charge with his French knights and mounted archers. Nevers and Coucy took command of the main body supporting the French knights while the Knights Hospitaller, Germans, and other allies remained with Sigismund and his Hungarian force.

The French cavalry attacked the Turkish militia and crushed them under the weight of their charge. The French fought their way into the next line of trained Turkish infantry (Janissaries) and began to take casualties from the withering bow fire and defensive stakes they encountered. Couchy and Vienne sent word that perhaps the French should retire to regroup and rest but their exuberance for battle and hope for victory pushed them forward into pursuit of the fleeing Turks. The French knights mounted and on foot chased after the Turks up a hill and when they reached the crest they realized that a fresh contingent of Sipahis were waiting for them. The Sipahis surged forward yelling "God is great!", and the Ottoman counterattack sent a large block of French knights reeling down the hill in full retreat while the rest stood their ground and fought on. Several knights were killed and Nevers along

Christian ships offer safe passage

with his bodyguard surrendered to the Turks. Witnessing Nevers taken hostage the rest of the French threw down their arms and capitulated.

The Sipahis counterattack pushed through and around the surrendering French. The Turks forward momentum along with a stampede of riderless horses confused the Hungarians and their allies. The Transylvanians and Wallachians assumed the day was lost and retired from the battlefield with the Hungarians and Germans continuing to fight in order to prevent a total massacre. Stefan Lazarević along with his 1,500 Serbian knights arrived at a critical juncture to push the fate of the battle safely into the hands of the Turks. Sigismund managed to escape on a fisherman's boat and Nikola II Gorjanski, Lazarević's brother-in-law, who was fighting under Sigismund, arranged the surrender of the remaining army.

The bloodshed did not end when the battle concluded as Sultan Bayezid separated the captors between nobles worthy of a ransom, young knights capable of being sold into slavery, and those who were to be executed. It took almost 2 years but finally the surviving leaders–Nevers, Boucicaut, Guillaume de Tremoille and Jacques de la Marche arrived back in France in February 1398. Western Europe was unable to stem the tide of theTurkish advances until the 1440's. Wallachia continued its resistance against the Turks and when Sultan Bayezid was captured in 1402 at Ankara the Ottoman Empire fell into chaos. The Battle of Nicopolis heavily influenced the dissolution of the Second Bulgarian Empire and the victors were able to prevent a united European coalition as well as maintaining a plausible threat on central Europe.

An Ottoman view of the battle of Nicopolis

The battle of Nicopolis 15th century painting

Wargaming the Battle of Nicopolis
Ratio- 1:1 (Turks: Christians)

Turks and Serbian Order of Battle: 12 units

Commanding Officers:
Sultan Bayezid I (Center), Prince Stefan Lazarević (Reserve), Doğan Bey (Vanguard)

Center	Vanguard	Reserve
3 units of infantry	3 units of light cavalry	1 unit of heavy cavalry
2 units of heavy cavalry	1 unit of missile infantry	2 units of light cavalry

Crusader Order of Battle: 12 units

Commanding Officers:
Sigismund (Center), Mircea cel Batran, the Elder (Left Flank), Stephen Laczkoivc (Right Flank)
John de Nevers (Vanguard), Nikola II Gorjanski (Reserve)

Right Flank	Left Flank	Center
1 unit of missile infantry	1 unit of infantry	2 units of heavy cavalry
1 unit of light cavalry	1 unit of light cavalry	1 unit of infantry

Vanguard	Reserve
2 units of heavy cavalry	2 units of infantry
1 unit of lightcavalry	

Battlefield Conditions

Defensive Stakes: The Turks had placed a wall of stakes along the length of their battle line and as the impetuous French knights drew close the Turks fell back behind the barricade causing the knights to dismount and begin removing the stakes. The stakes may be placed behind the vanguard of the Turks and cavalry cannot pass through the obstacle unless they dismount.

Serbian Reserves: Prince Stefan Lazarević held his cavalry in an ambush and at the opportune time he lunged into battle. Stefan and his units are held in reserve off the table and at the start of any turn the Turkish player may deploy the Serbians along their table edge.

The Commanders

Sigismund of Luxemburg (14 February 1368 – 9 December 1437) was Prince-elector of Brandenburg from 1378 until 1388 and from 1411 until 1415, King of Hungary and Croatia from 1387, King of Germany from 1411, King of Bohemia from 1419, King of Italy from 1431, and Holy Roman Emperor for four years from 1433 until 1437, the last male member of the House of Luxemburg. He was regarded as highly educated, spoke several languages (among them French, German, Hungarian, Italian, and Latin) and was an outgoing person who also took pleasure in the tournament. Sigismund was one of the driving forces behind the Council of Constance that ended the Papal Schism, but which in the end also led to the Hussite Wars that dominated the later period of Sigismund's life. He was buried in Nagyvárad, Kingdom of Hungary (now Oradea, Romania).

Bayezid I "The Lightning" (1360 – 8 March 1403) was the Sultan of the Ottoman Empire from 1389 to 1402. He was the son of Murad I and Gülçiçek Hatun. Bayezid ascended to the throne following the death of his father Murad I, who was killed by Serbian knight Miloš Obilić during (15 June), or immediately after (16 June), the Battle of Kosovo in 1389, by which Serbia became a vassal of the Ottoman Empire. Immediately after obtaining the throne, he had his younger brother strangled to avoid a plot. In 1390, Bayezid took as a wife Princess Olivera Despina, the daughter of Prince Lazar of Serbia, who also lost his life in Kosovo. Bayezid recognized Stefan Lazarević, the son of Lazar, as the new Serbian leader (later despot), with considerable autonomy. Thus, the siege of Constantinople continued, lasting until 1402. The beleaguered Byzantines had their reprieve when Bayezid fought the Timurid Empire in the East. At this time, the empire of Bayezid included Thrace (except Constantinople), Macedonia, Bulgaria, and parts of Serbia in Europe. In Asia, his domains extended to the Taurus Mountains. His army was considered one of the best in the Islamic world. In 1400, the Central Asian warlord Timur succeeded in rousing the local Turkic beyliks that had been vassals of the Ottomans to join him in his attack on Bayezid, who was also considered one of the most powerful rulers in the Muslim world during that period. In the fateful Battle of Ankara, on 20 July 1402, Bayezid was captured by Timur and the Ottoman army was defeated. Many writers claim that Bayezid was mistreated by the Timurids. However, writers and historians from Timur's own court reported that Bayezid was treated well, and that Timur even mourned his death. One of Bayezid's sons, Mustafa Çelebi, was captured with him and held captive in Samarkand until 1405.

Sigismund of Luxemburg

Bayezid I

Battle of Shrewsbury

Date: 21 July 1403
Where: Shrewsbury, Shropshire, England

Opponents:
Kingdom of England – approximately 14,000 men
Rebel Forces – approximately 11,000 men

Background:

Henry IV, supported by the Percy family, became embroiled in a civil war with Richard II over the English throne. In 1399 Henry took the throne and was supported by the Percys in several conflicts in both Wales and Scotland. The promise of titles, land, and money were offered by King Henry IV in exchange for the lord's support; when the wars ended the lands around Cumberland that were promised to the Percys were given to a rival. This insult was enough to convince Henry Percy to rebel against their king along with the Earls of Northumberland and Worcester. In Percy's mind, the revolt was justified because of the following reasons: King Henry lied to the nobles when he offered them land in exchange for the throne; Henry taxed the clergy even when he promised he would not without the consent of Parliament; Henry imprisoned and murdered the former King Richard II; and Henry refused to allow Parliament a free election.

In July 1403, Henry Percy assembled a force of about 200 retainers and moved south to meet up with his uncle, Thomas Percy, 1st Earl of Worcester. When the Percys arrived in Cheshire, an area known to despise Henry IV, they recruited the bulk of their army including the Cheshire archers that fought as Richard II's bodyguard.

King Henry IV was unaware of these developments until he received word on 12 July ironically while he was marching north to rendezvous with the Percys to fight the Scots. He immediately changed his plans to intercept the Percys and put an end to the rebellion. The army under King Henry shifted westwards and marched towards Shrewsbury arriving before the Percys could capture the town. Both forces arrived on 20 July and established their camps on the north and south banks of the Sevem River. The following morning King Henry shifted his army eastward about a mile and crossed the River Sevem with the hopes of cutting off the Percys line of retreat to Chester.

The two armies lined up in a large field of growing peas and for most of the morning on Saturday 21 July the leaders parlayed inconclusively. The Percy's and King Henry returned to their respective armies and about two hours before dusk King Henry raised his sword and huge volleys of arrows were loosed by both sides. Casualties mounted on both sides and Percy's Cheshire bowmen proved to be the better archers collapsing the King's right wing and forcing them from the field. The King's left wing led by Henry, Prince of Wales, remained relatively intact and held firm against the onslaught. Henry Percy seized the opportunity seeing the King's

Henry IV leads troops to battle

army falter and charged hoping to kill the King and end the battle. During the attempt Henry Percy was killed when he opened the visor on his helmet and was shot in the face. Northumbrian knights falsely celebrated the death of King Henry IV and shouted 'Henry Percy King!', but the statement was retaliated by the king himself saying 'Henry Percy is dead!'. Since there was no reply both sides understood that Henry Percy was indeed dead and not the king. With the contender for the crown dead the battle ended even though the King's forces sustained greater casualties and the King himself almost lost his life.

During the battle Sir Walter Blount, the Royal Standard bearer, was killed by Archibald Douglas, 4th Earl of Douglas. On the following day many of the leaders in Percy's army were hanged, drawn and quartered in the town of Shrewsbury. Thomas Percy, 1st Earl of Worcester, Sir Richard Venables, Sir Richard Vemon and Sir Henry Boynton all lost their lives attempting to place Henry Percy on the throne. Henry Percy was buried with honors at Whitchurch, Shropshire but rumors quickly surfaced that he was still alive so King Henry IV had his body disinterred. King Henry put his body on display in Shrewsbury and eventually had his head sent to York and his body parts sent to Chester, London, Bristol and Newcastle upon Tyne. Henry IV continued to defend his throne including the Glyndwr uprising in Wales, and several invasions from Northern England. He ended up serving as King for ten more years before he died on March 20, 1413.

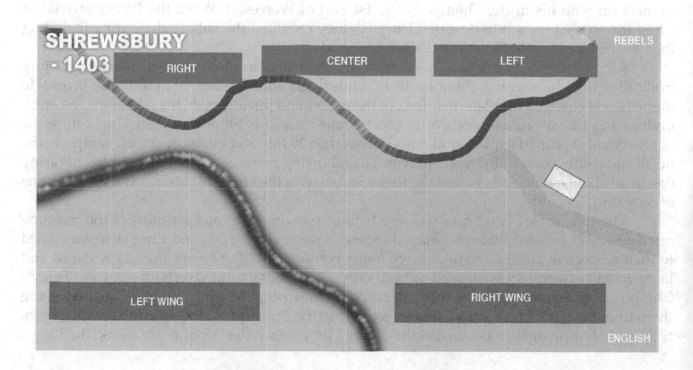

Wargaming the Battle of Shrewsbury
Ratio- 3:2 (English: Rebels)

English Order of Battle: 15 units

Commanding Officer:
Henry IV of England (Right Wing); Henry, Prince of Wales (Left Wing)

Right Wing
4 units of missile infantry
2 units of heavy cavalry
2 units of infantry

Left Wing
4 units of missile infantry
2 units of heavy cavalry
1 unit of infantry

Rebel Order of Battle: 10 units

Commanding Officer:
Henry "Harry Hotspur" Percy, Thomas Percy

Right Flank
2 units of missile infantry
1 unit of infantry

Left Flank
2 units of missile infantry
1 unit of infantry

Center
2 units of missile infantry
2 units of infantry

Battlefield Conditions

Death of the King: A false claim of King Henry's death was exclaimed during the battle but it was actually Henry Percy who was killed. Once the rebels realized they lost their king apparent they withdrew from the field. If either King Henry or Henry Percy are killed then the battle ends immediately.

The attack on the rebel camp

The death of Hotspur

The Commanders

Henry IV (15 April 1367 – 20 March 1413) was King of England and Lord of Ireland from 1399 to 1413 and asserted the claim of his grandfather, Edward III, to the Kingdom of France. He was born at Bolingbroke Castle in Lincolnshire, hence his other name, Henry of Bolingbroke. His father, John of Gaunt, was the third son of Edward III, and enjoyed a position of considerable influence during much of the reign of Henry's cousin Richard II, whom Henry eventually deposed. Henry's mother was Blanche, heiress to the considerable Lancaster estates, and thus he became the first King of England from the Lancaster branch of the Plantagenets. Henry spent much of his reign defending himself against plots, rebellions and assassination attempts.

Sir Henry Percy (20 May 1364 – 21 July 1403), commonly known as Sir Harry Hotspur, or simply Hotspur, was a late medieval English nobleman. He was known as one of the most valiant knights of his day and a significant captain during the Anglo-Scottish wars. He later led successive rebellions against Henry IV of England and was slain at the Battle of Shrewsbury in 1403 at the height of his career. Despite honors initially showered on the Percy's, they began to have a falling out over their defense of the Scottish border and guerilla war along the Welsh border. The Percys rebelled in the summer of 1403 in collusion with the Welsh leader Glyndŵr. On his return to England shortly after the victory at Homildon Hill, Henry Percy issued proclamations in Cheshire accusing the king of 'tyrannical government'. Joined by his uncle, Thomas Percy, Earl of Worcester, he marched to Shrewsbury, where he intended to engage the forces there under the command of the Prince of Wales. His father's troops, however, did not arrive in time and Sir Henry decided to continue on to Shrewsbury on 21 July 1403, where they encountered the king with a large army. The ensuing Battle of Shrewsbury was fierce, with heavy casualties on both sides, but when Henry Percy was killed, his troops fled. When rumors began to circulate after the battle that Percy was still alive, the king 'had the corpse exhumed and displayed it, propped upright between two millstones, in the market place at Shrewsbury'. Afterwards, Percy's head was sent to York, where it was impaled on the Micklegate Bar (one of the city's gates), whereas his four-quarters were sent to London, Newcastle upon Tyne, Bristol, and Chester before they were finally delivered to his widow. She had him buried in York Minster. In January 1404, Percy was posthumously declared a traitor, and his lands were forfeited to the Crown.

Henry IV

The death of Henry Percy

Battle of Grunwald

AKA: *First Battle of Tannenberg, Battle of Žalgiris*
Date: 15 July 15 1410
Where: Between the villages of Grunwald and
                 Stębark in present day Poland

Opponents:
Kingdom of Poland and Grand Duchy of Lithuania
                 – approximately 39,000 men
Teutonic Order – approximately 27,000 men

Background:
About two hundred years before the Battle of Grunwald in 1230, the Teutonic Knights launched a Crusade against the pagan Prussian clans at the invitation of Conrad of Masovia. By 1280 the Prussians had been conquered and converted to Christianity so attention shifted to the pagan Grand Duchy of Lithuania. The Teutonic Order raided and attacked Lithuania for almost a hundred years but made very little progress. Also during that time, the Order was at odds with the Crown of Poland as they attempted to re-establish control of their fractured realm. In 1385, the Grand Duke Jogaila of Lithuania married Queen Jadwiga of Poland and converted to Christianity forming a union between the two realms and taking the name of Władysław II Jagiełło. This transformation of Lithuania's religious beliefs removed any reason for the Teutonic Knights to invade the realm but Grandmaster Conrad Zöllner von Rothenstein challenged the sincerity of the conversion and brought the issue to the papal court. The situation continued to fester as both Poland and Lithuania made territorial claims against the Teutonic Order as well as requested trade considerations since the knights controlled the lower parts of the three largest rivers in the area (Neman, Vistula, Daugava).

King Jagiello (Testudo Miniatures)

Teutonic Banner Bearer (Testudo Miniatures)

Polish Knights (Molniya Miniatures)

Teutonic Standard Bearer (Testudo Miniatures)

In May 1409, an uprising occurred in the Teutonic held territory of Samogitia and the Lithuanians supported the cause. The knights threatened to invade Lithuania causing Poland to side with its neighbor and announced its preparations to attack Prussia. On 6 August 1409 Grand Master Ulrich von Jungingen decalred war on both, the Kingdom of Poland and the Grand Duchy ofLithuania. The Teutonic Order wanted to deal with its enemy's separately beginning with an invasion of Poland. Several towns and castles were sacked or burned by the knights and Polish forces counterattacked but neither side was prepared for a full-scale war. Wenceslaus, King of the Romans mediated the dispute with a truce signed on 8 October 1409 and its expiration date set for 24 June 1410. The treaty gave all the forces involved time to prepare for the inevitable war as well as engage in foreign diplomatic positioning.

By December 1409, Władysław and Vytautas agreed to mass their forces and march towards the capital of the Teutonic Knights, Marienburg. Ulrich von Jungingen concentrated his army in a central location with the ability to react quickly to the logical attack routes of both Poland and Lithuania. Władysław and Vytautas had their forces perform borders raids pinning

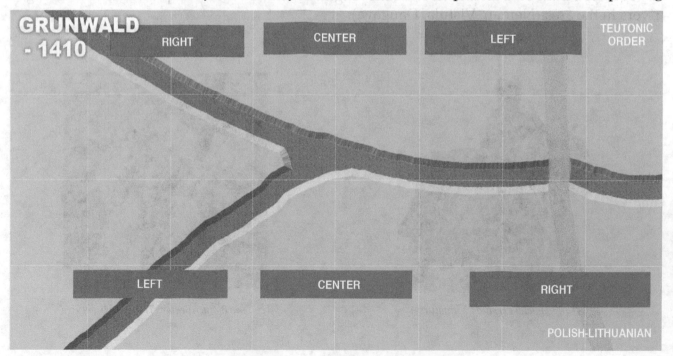

the Teutonic army in place in preparation for a massed attack that the Teutonic Order did not anticipate.

The Polish-Lithuanian forces began their marches in early June and worked their way towards Czerwinsk, the pre-arranged meeting place approximately 80 km from the Prussian border. By the time all the forces arrived and crossed the Vistula River it was 3 July with the army crossing into Prussia on 9 July. Once Ulrich von Jungingen received notification that the Polish-Lithuanian army had moved into Prussia he organized his forces and established a defensive line on the Drewenz River near the town of Kauemik. Władysław elected to avoid a river crossing against a strong defensible position so he chose to circumvent the crossing and find an easier path towards Marienburg. The Teutonic army shadowed their enemy along the Drewenz River and after the Polish-Lithuanian force sacked the village of Gilgenburg, von Jungingen vowed the destruction of the invaders.

The two armies deployed in the early morning of 15 July 1410 with the Polish-Lithuanian force positioned in the front and east of the towns of Ludwigsdorf and Tannenberg. The Polish heavy cavalry anchored the left flank, the Lithuanian light cavalry positioned on the right flank and the various mercenary troops formed the middle. The invaders were organized in three lines of wedge-shaped formations with each unit consisting of about 20 men. On the other side of the battlefield the Teutonic forces stationed their elite cavalry under the command of Grand Marshal Frederic von Wallenrode directly across from the Lithuanian light cavalry.

Polish Knights (Molniya Miniatures)

Lithuanian Infantry (Molniya Miniatures)

The armies faced each other for several hours waiting for the other side to begin the attack. Von Wallenrode sent messengers with two swords to Władysław and Vytautas hoping to provoke them into attacking. Vytautas began the battle and charged his cavalry forward supported by a few Polish units. After more than an hour of heavy fighting, the Lithuanian force turned and fled from the battlefield with the Knights in hot pursuit. During the Lithuanian rout heavy fighting broke out along the rest of the line; Grand Komtur Kunovon Lichtenstein launched a punishing charge against the Polish right flank.

During the Teutonic pursuit of the Lithuanian army, six banners broke off and joined von Lichtenstein's attack in an attempt to capture the royal banner of Kraków. The banner was temporarily captured but Polish forces quickly regained the royal flag. Władysław ordered his second line into battle to support the melee and at the same time Grand Master Ulrich von Jungingen led sixteen banners of men, almost a third of the army, to press the attack on the Polish right flank. During the height of the engagement the Lithuanian army returned to battle and attacked the rear of the Teutonic force. Von Jungingen attempted to break through the Lithuanian lines but was killed in the process leaving the Teutonic army leaderless. The knights were outnumbered and lacking a leader resulted in several units retreating back to their camp. Unfortunately for the Teutonic knights the camp followers turned against their masters and forced the survivors into a wagon fort which was quickly broken and destroyed. The knights were slaughtered on the battlefield after a ten hour long engagement.

The Battle of Grunwald was one of the largest battles in Medieval Europe and viewed as one of the most important victories in the history of Poland, Belarus, and Lithuania. The events surrounding the battle became stories of legend and a moment of national pride for the victors. The "Grunwald Swords" delivered to Władysław and Vytautas were intended as an insult and later after the victory the swords became a national symbol of Poland. The battle was used as propaganda by Germany, Lithuania, Poland, and Russia for generations to come and played an important part in political maneuvering especially during World War I and World War II.

Polish Archers (Molniya Miniatures)

Early Handgunners (Molniya Miniatures)

Wargaming the Battle of Grunwald
Ratio- 3:2 (Polish/Lithuanian: TeutonicOrder)

Polish-Lithuanian Order of Battle: 18 units

Commanding Officer:
Władysław II Jagiełło, Vytautas the Great

Right Flank	**Left Flank**	**Center**
3 units of heavy cavalry	3 units of heavy cavalry	3 units of heavy cavalry
1 unit of light cavalry	1 unit of light cavalry	3 units of infantry
		3 units of missile infantry

Teutonic Order of Battle: 12 units

Commanding Officer:
Grandmaster Ulrich von Jungingen (Right Flank), Marshal Frederic von Wallenrode (Left Flank), Grand Komtur Kuno von Lichtenstein (Center)

Right Flank	**Left Flank**	**Center**
3 units of heavy cavalry	3 units of heavy cavalry	3 units of heavy cavalry
		1 unit of missile infantry
		2 units of infantry

Battlefield Conditions

None: The Battle of Grunwald was one of the largest medieval battles and was a pitched battle of two massive armies with a large amount of cavalry.

The Battle of Grunwald by Jan Matejko

The Commanders

Jogaila, later ***Władysław II Jagiełło*** (c. 1352/1362 – 1 June 1434) was Grand Duke of Lithuania (1377–1434), King of Poland (1386–1399) alongside his wife Jadwiga, and then sole King of Poland until his own death. He ruled in Lithuania from 1377. Born a pagan, he converted to Catholicism in 1386 and was baptized as Władysław in Kraków, married the young Queen Jadwiga, and was crowned King of Poland as Władysław II Jagiełło. In 1387 he converted Lithuania to Christianity. His own reign in Poland started in 1399, upon the death of Queen Jadwiga, and lasted a further thirty-five years which laid the foundation for the centuries-long Polish–Lithuanian union. He was the founder of the Jagiellonian dynasty in Poland that bears his name and was the heir to the already established house of Gediminids in the Grand Duchy of Lithuania. These royal dynasties ruled both states until 1572 and then through the female line until 1668. The Jagiellonians became one of the most influential dynasties in the late medieval and early modern Central and Eastern Europe. During his reign, the Polish-Lithuanian state was the largest state in the Christian world.

Ulrich von Jungingen (8 January 1360 – 15 July 1410) was the 26th Grand Master of the Teutonic Knights, serving from 1407 to 1410. His policy of confrontation with the Grand Duchy of Lithuania and the Kingdom of Poland would spark the Polish–Lithuanian–Teutonic War and lead to disaster for his Order, and his own death, at the Battle of Grunwald. Ulrich received no help from his ally King Sigismund, who was completely involved in another conflict with his cousin Jobst of Moravia over the election as King of the Romans. Ulrich tried to shame his opponents to battle at Grunwald by sending over two swords to the Polish commanders. According Jan Długosz, he was met and defeated by the Polish knight Mszczuj of Skrzynno. King Jogaila allowed his body to be sent to Malbork Castle before he began the Siege of Marienburg.

Ulrich von Jungingen (Matejko detail)

King Jagiello (Contemporary)

Battle of Agincourt

Date: 25 October 1415
Where: Agincourt, Pas-de-Calais, France

Opponents:
England – approximately 7,500 men
France – approximately 15,000 men

Background:

The Battle of Agincourt took place during the Hundred Years War on Saint Crispin's Day, 25 October 1415 after a long and drawn out negotiation failed between England and France. Henry V, King of England, claimed the crown of France for his own and through recommendations of his council he entered into peaceful negotiations in the spring of 1414. Henry V offered that he would remove his claim on the crown if France paid their outstanding debt of 1.6 million crowns for the ransom of John II; conceded ownership over Normandy, Touraine, Anjou, Brittany, Flanders and Aquitaine; and allowed Charles VI's daughter Princess Catherine to marry him as well as pay a dowry of 2 million crowns. France made a counter offer which was considered an insult and by 19 April 1415 Henry V and England declared war on France.

Henry V led the invasion of France himself and after several months of preparations the English landed and laid siege to the port city of Harfleur on 13 August 1415. The city fell after a month on 22 September but the English forces were not prepared to depart until 8 October. The campaign season was rapidly coming to a close and with only one city taken as well as a sick and starving army; Henry decided to march to the English stronghold of Calais. This maneuver served to demonstrate Henry's rule over the duchy of Normandy, his claim to the French throne, and prod Louis, Dauphin of France and Duke of Guyenne into a fight.

Whiile the siege of Harfleur was underway the French were mobilizing but were unable to raise enough troops in time to challenge the English and lift the siege. As Henry marched his army north the French shadowed their movements and by 24 October they faced each other for battle.The French were reluctant to engage and delayed, hoping to acquire more troops but on the morning of 25 October, Henry poised his troops for battle.

The English deployed across a 750 yard defile into three 'battles' or divisions under the commands of Edward of Norwich, 2nd Duke of York; King Henry V; and Thomas de Camoys, 1st Baron Camoys. Approximately 7,000 longbowmen deployed on the flanks of these battles with about 1,500 men-at-arms and knights making up the center. The archers deployed stakes in front of their positions to protect themselves as well as drive the

English infantry of Agincourt

horses towards the center of the battlefield.

The French force had a numerical advantage over the British and arrayed themselves into three lines. The first line consisting of approximately 4,000-8,000 men-at-arms, 4,000 archers, and 1,500 crossbowmen was led by Constable D'Albret; Jean Le Maingre, Marshal Boucicault; Charles, Duke of Orléans; and Jean de Bourbon, Duke of Bourbon. Attached to the first line were two 'wings' of around 600-800 men-at-arms and cavalry which was under the command of Louis, Count of Vendôme and Sir Clignet de Brebant. The second line was almost identical in numbers to the first line and was under the leadership of Edward III, Duke of Bar; Jean I, Duke of Alençon; and Philip II, Count of Nevers. The third line consisted mostly of peasants, servants, and commoners armed with various weapons but not much is known about their numbers since they did not see any fighting. The third line was commanded by the Counts of Dammartin and Fauconberg.

The morning of 25 October 1415 the French army stood idle and was patiently waiting for the arrival of reinforcements. The Dukes of Brabant, Anjou, and Brittany were still marching towards the battle site with almost 10,000 men. The French were in no rush to engage the English since they blocked their intended destination of Calais. King Henry was concerned about the state of his army. He knew needed to force the French to action so the archers pulled up their stakes and the English marched forward to establish a new position closer to the French vanguard. The French knights continued to observe as the English longbowmen prepared their new positions and at 300 yards the opening volley of arrows began to rain upon the French lines.

The French cavalry were spurred into action and began a headlong charge into the English archers but the flanks were protected by woods and their front was defended by stakes making a direct charge a disaster from the onset. The casualties mounted and the already muddy landscape was further disturbed by the trampling horses. The French infantry advance became slightly disordered by the retreating knights as they began their long advance toward the English lines in heavy armor through thick muddy ground. The two forces collided and the

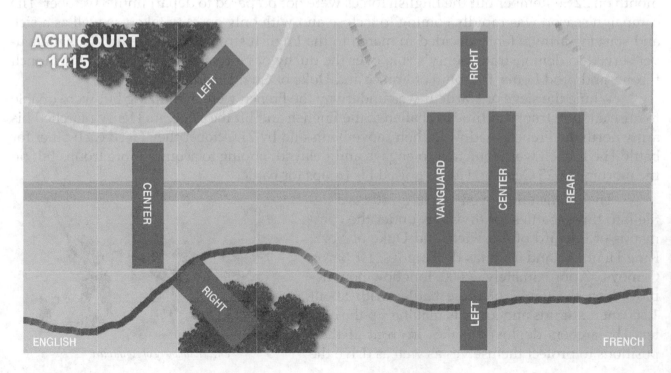

French initially made progress pushing back the English but were quickly exhausted and unable to prolong the attack. The more lightly armored English troops seized the advantage and began to overtake the French. The situation was further worsened when French reinforcements moved into action pinning the already engaged troops and forcing the new arrivals to fight over the fallen of their comrades. The outcome of the battle was decisive and the estimated casualties for the French were staggering. Thousands of French lay dead in the mud with thousands more put to the sword after their capture. King Henry returned to England a conquering hero but it wasn't until 1420 with the signing of the Treaty of Troyes and Henry's marriage to Catherine of Valois when his claim to the French throne was secured.

Wargaming the Battle of Agincourt
Ratio- 2:1 (French: English)

French Order of Battle: 16 units

Commanding Officers:
Constable D'Albret, Jean Le Maingre, Marshal Boucicault; Charles, Duke of Orléans; Jean de Bourbon, Duke of Bourbon (Vanguard), Louis, Count of Vendôme and Sir Clignet de Brebant (Left & Right Flanks), Edward III, Duke of Bar; Jean I, Duke of Alençon; and Philip II, Count of Nevers (Center), Counts of Dammartin and Fauconberg (Rear)

Right Flank
2 units of heavy cavalry

Left Flank
2 units of heavy cavalry

Center
2 units of infantry
2 units of missile infantry

Vanguard
2 units of infantry
2 units of missile infantry

Rear
3 units of infantry
1 unit of missile infantry

English Order of Battle: 8 units

Commanding Officers:
King Henry V (Center), Edward of Norwich, 2nd Duke of York (Right Flank), Thomas de Camoys, 1st Baron Camoys (Left Flank)

Right Flank
2 units of missile infantry
with defensive stakes
1 unit of infantry

Left Flank
2 units of missile infantry
with defensive stakes
1 unit of infantry

Center
2 units of infantry

Battlefield Conditions

Muddy Ground: Arguably the most influential factor of the battle was the landscape and its muddy conditions which played a huge role in the outcome. Some games may already have rules to govern muddy ground considering the movement difficult or slow going. The players may want to increase the difficulty as more and more troops move over the ground. This could possibly encourage the French to deploy their cavalry in the first wave taking advantage of their faster moving troops.

French Problems: The French superior numbers were historically nullified because of the narrow battlefield which forced them to deploy their army in waves. Players may want to create a similar condition where the French army is only allowed to deploy a portion of their force with the rest held off table in reserve. The Rear units really did not play an active role in the battle so players may want to ignore these troops altogether. Historically, the majority of the French troops armed with bows or crossbows were held behind the men-at-arms and cavalry reducing their effectiveness during the battle. The French side could be given set marching orders unable to alter how their army deploys or the French players could be given the freedom to adjust their deployment based on situation of the day.

English Tactics: The English forces were greatly outnumbered but elected to take the fight to the French in a narrow stretch of land greatly reducing the French advantage. The English deployment could be in a more open area with the bottleneck located closer to the French lines. The English player could incorporate rules allowing the archers to redeploy their stakes or the game can begin with the English already in their final positions. The longbow should have a shooting range greater than any other bow or crossbow and to encourage the French to attack swiftly the French forces could start in longbow range from the start of the game. The muddy terrain should be a movement hindrance to the English but the more lightly armed troops should be less hampered than the more heavily armed troops.

A line of English archers await the French

French and English troops (Perry Miniatures)

The Commanders

Henry V (9 August 1387 – 31 August 1422) was King of England from 1413 until his death at the age of 35 in 1422. He was the second English monarch who came from the House of Lancaster. After gaining military experience fighting the Welsh during the revolt of Owain Glyn Dwr, and against the powerful aristocratic Percys of Northumberland at the Battle of Shrewsbury, Henry came into political conflict with his father, whose health was increasingly precarious from 1405 onward. After his father's death in 1413, Henry assumed control of the country and embarked on a war with France in the ongoing Hundred Years' War (1337–1453). His military successes culminated in his famous victory at the Battle of Agincourt (1415) and saw him come close to conquering France. After months of negotiation with Charles VI of France, the Treaty of Troyes (1420) recognized Henry V as regent and heir-apparent to the French throne, and he was subsequently married to Charles's daughter, Catherine of Valois (1401–37). Following Henry V's sudden and unexpected death in France two years later, he was succeeded by his infant son, who reigned as Henry VI (1422–61, 1470–71).

Charles d'Albret (died 25 October 1415) was Constable of France from 1402 until 1411, and again from 1413 until 1415. He was also the co-commander of the French army at the Battle of Agincourt where he was killed by the English forces led by King Henry V. Charles was born into an old Gascon family, the son of Arnaud, Lord of Albret, and Margaret de Bourbon.[1] He fought under Bertrand du Guesclin as a young man. He was made the constable of France by Charles VI in 1402, but was dismissed when the Burgundian faction gained power at court. He was restored to his office in 1413 when the Armagnac faction regained power.

The arms of Charles d'Albret

Henry V

Battle of Varna

Date: 10 November 1444
Where: Varna, Bulgaria

Opponents:

Kingdom of Poland, Kingdom of Hungary, Kingdom of Croatia, Crown of Bohemia, Wallachia, Bulgarian rebels, Papal States, Teutonic Knights –
approximately 22,000 men

Ottoman Empire – approximately 50,000 men

Background:

In 1437 King Sigismund died and the Hungarian Kingdom fell into disarray. Sigismund's son-in-law, Albert, took the throne but only ruled for two years before he died in 1439 leaving his wife Elizabeth with an unborn child. The Hungarian nobles asked Władysław III of Poland to become King of Hungary and aid in the defense against the Ottomans. From the moment of Władysław's coronation he never returned to Poland and alongside the influential nobleman, John Hunyadi, he took over the rule of the Hungarian Kingdom.

The Ottomans launched an invasion against Hungary from 1440-1442, but failed to take Belgrade and Transylvania. The failures of their campaigns from 1440-1442 along with their defeats from the 'long campaign' resulted in the Ottoman sultan Murad II signing a ten year truce with Hungary. With the peace treaty signed Murad resigned the throne and his twelve year old son Mehmed II became the new sultan.

Władysław along with John Hunyadi anticipated a renewed offensive by Mehmed and offered to lead a crusading army after establishing an alliance with Venice and Pope Eugene IV. Mehmed received the news of the coalition forming against him and realizing his inexperience he asked his father to return to the throne and lead theTurks into battle, but Murad II declined. Angered, Mehmed wrote his father a letter saying, 'If you are the Sultan, come and lead your armies. If I am the Sultan I hereby order you to come and lead my armies." After Murad II received this letter he returned to lead the Ottoman army against the Christians.

The Papal army was comprised of Hungarian, Polish, Bohemian and Wallachian soldiers totaling around 22,000 men. The army also consisted of smaller detachments of Czechs, Papal knights, Teutonic knights, Bosnians, Croatians, Bulgarians, Lithuanians and Ukrainians. The plan was put in place to send this force toward Varna where it would board Papal, Venetian, and Genoese ships and sail to Constantinople with hopes of pushing the Turks out of Europe. The Christians moved rapidly, bypassing several Ottoman fortresses and allowing the Bulgarians to join the crusade.

The Ottomans deployed an army of around 50,000 men towards Varna from the west on 9 November. Shocked by the size of the Ottoman army Hunyadi called a military council to decide the next move. Papal legate, Cardinal Julian Cesarini suggested a hasty withdrawal but the Black Sea, Lake Varna, the wooded slopes of the Franga plateau and the arrivingTurks pre-

Cavalry forces meet

vented a retreat. Hunyadi declared, 'To escape is impossible, to surrender is unthinkable' and Władysław agreed with the philosophy giving Hunyadi full command of the Christian force.

On the morning of 10 November, Hunyadi positioned the army in an arc between Lake Varna and the Franga plateau. Władysław's Polish and Hungarian bodyguards, royal mercenaries, and the Hungarian nobles totaling around 3,500 men deployed in the center with the Wallachian cavalry held in reserve behind the main force. The right flank of the army with approximately 6,500 soldiers was stationed on a hill towards the village of Kamenar. Bishop Jan Dominek of Varadin commanded the flank with Cesarini leading German and Bosnian mercenaries, Bishop of Eger commanding the papal troops, and Ban Franco Talotsi, governor of Slavonia, in charge of a contingent of Croatians. The left flank consisted of 5,000 men and was commanded by Michael Szilágyi, Hunyadi's brother-in-law, who led Transylvanians, Bulgarians, German mercenaries and Hungarian magnates. Behind the Hungarians and closer to the Black Sea, Hetman Ceyka was in charge of the Wagenburg (wagon forts) equipped with bombards. He deployed about 300-600 Czech and Ukrainian mercenaries along with Poles, Lithuanians, and Wallachians to man the series of wagon forts with about 7-10 soldiers for each wagon.

The Ottoman center displayed itself around two Thracian burial mounds and consisted of Janissaries (elite infantry) as well as levies from Rumelia. The center established a defensive position digging ditches and building two palisades to fight behind. Murad was stationed on one of the burial mounds giving him a high vantage point from which to observe the impending battle. The right wing of the Turks were Kapikulus (slave infantry) and Sipahis (cavalry) also from Rumelia and the left wing was comprised of Akıncıs (irregular light cavalry), Sipahis from

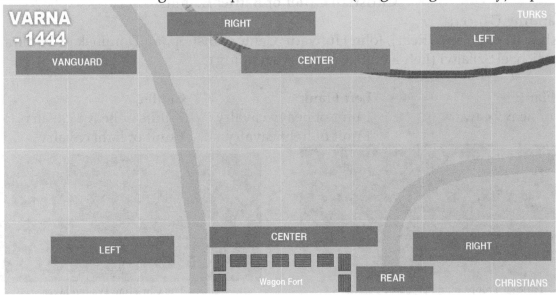

Anatolia as well as additional troops. Murad also deployed an advanced force of Janissary archers and Akıncıs on the Franga plateau.

The battle kicked off when the Ottoman Akıncıs assaulted the Croats led by Ban Talotsi and the Christians unloaded their bombards and firearms to repulse the attack. As the Ottomans retreated the Croats pursued them in a disorganized manner allowing them to be ambushed in the flank by fresh Anatolian cavalry. The Christian right flank tried to withdrawal toward the small fortress of Galata on the opposite side of Varna Bay but the deadly Ottoman ambush cut down several of the Christians including Cesarini in the marshland around Varna Lake. The only troops to survive the onslaught were Ban Talotsi's who were able to withdraw behind the safety of the Wagenburg.

On the opposite flank, the Turks charged into the Hungarians and Bulgarians led by Szilágyi and were repulsed but the Sipahis regrouped and attacked a second time. Hunyadi wanted to support the left flank so with two cavalry companies he left the center advising Władysław to hold the middle until he returned. Ignoring Hunyadi's advice Władysław led 500 Polish knights against the Turkish center pushing through the Janissary infantry and almost succeeded in taking Murad prisoner. Władysław fell off his horse outside of Murad's tent and was beheaded by Janissary bodyguards. The rest of the Polish cavalry suffered a similar fate and were massacred by the Ottomans. When Hunyadi returned to the center he attempted unsuccessfully to recover the king's body and then orchestrated a retreat for the remnants of the army.

The death of Władysław put the Hungarian throne in the hands of four year old Ladislaus V, the Posthumous, of Bohemia and Hungary forcing Hungary to recover from its losses. The Turkish victory eliminated a significant European threat and allowed more territory to fall under the Ottoman Empire. The Battle of Varna had a direct impact on the fall of Constantinople in 1453 changing the events of Turkish influence for future generations.

Wargaming the Battle of Varna
Ratio- 1:2 (Christians:Turks)

Christian Order of Battle: 12 units

Commanding Officer:
Władyslaw III of Poland (Rear), John Hunyadi (Center), Bishop Jan Dominek of Varadin (Right Flank), Michael Szilágyi (Left Flank), Ceyka (Wagenburg)

Right Flank	**Left Flank**	**Center**
3 units of heavy cavalry	1 unit of heavy cavalry	3 units of heavy cavalry
	1 unit of light cavalry	1 unit of light cavalry

Turkish Troops man defensive positions

The Christian Wagen lager

Rear
2 units of light cavalry

Wagenburg
1 unit of infantry equipped with handguns
and bombards defending a wagonfort

Turks Order of Battle: 24 units

Commanding Officer:
Murad II (Center), Karadzsa (Left Flank), Turahán (Right Flank)

Right Flank
2 units of infantry (Kapikulus)
4 units of heavy cavalry (Sipahis)
2 units of light cavalry (Akıncıs)

Left Flank
4 units of heavy cavalry (Sipahis)
2 units of light cavalry (Akıncıs)

Center
2 units of missile infantry (Janissaries)
1 unit of light cavalry (Akıncıs)
1 unit of heavy cavalry (Guard)

Vanguard
2 units of missile infantry (Janissaries)
6 units of light cavalry (Akıncıs)

Battlefield Conditions

Wagenburg: The Wagenburg is essentially a fortification built by encircling the supply wagons and using them as a staunch defense. The Wagenburg is manned by soldiers equipped with handguns and manning bombard cannons. The Wagenburg can be represented by stretching it along the Christians deployment area allowing enough room for any withdrawing Christians to move behind the defenses.

Defenses: The Turks anchored their army on the center of their force defending ditches and palisades. The 2 units of missile infantry in the center will be placed behind the palisades with ditches in the front. The exact positioning of the missile infantry is determined by the player so the ditches and palisades will be placed after the missile infantry have been deployed. This will give them some added protection and bonuses against charging units.

The Christian line charges the Turkish encampment

Forces engage at Varna

The Commanders

Murad II Kodja or *Amurathes II* (June 1404, Amasya – 3 February 1451, Edirne)) was the Sultan of the Ottoman Empire from 1421 to 1451 (except for a period from 1444 to 1446 when his son Mehmed II reigned). Murad II's reign was marked by the long war he fought against the Christian feudal lords of the Balkans and the Turkish emirates in Anatolia, a conflict that lasted 25 years. He was brought up in Amasya, and ascended the throne on the death of his father Mehmed I. His mother was Valide Sultan Emine Hatun (daughter of Suleyman Bey, ruler of Dulkadirids), his father's third consort. Their marriage served as an alliance between the Ottomans and this buffer state. Murad II then formed a new army called Azeb in 1421 and marched through the Byzantine Empire and laid siege to its capital Constantinople. While Murad was besieging the city, the Byzantines, in league with some independent Turkish Anatolian states, sent the sultan's younger brother Mustafa (who was only 13 years old) to rebel against the sultan and besiege Bursa. Murad had to abandon the siege of Constantinople in order to deal with his rebellious brother. He caught Prince Mustafa and executed him. The Anatolian states that had been constantly plotting against him — Aydinids, Germiyanids, Menteshe and Teke — were annexed and henceforth became part of the Ottoman Empire.

Murad II then declared war against Venice, the Karamanid Emirate, Serbia and Hungary. The Karamanids were defeated in 1428 and Venice withdrew in 1432 following the defeat at the second Siege of Thessalonica in 1430. In the 1430s Murad captured vast territories in the Balkans and succeeded in annexing Serbia in 1439. In 1441 the Holy Roman Empire and Poland joined the Serbian-Hungarian coalition. In 1448 he defeated the Christian coalition at the Second Battle of Kosovo (the first one took place in 1389). When the Balkan front was secured, Murad II turned east to defeat Timur's son, Shah Rokh, and the emirates of Karamanid and Çorum-Amasya. In 1450 Murad II led his army into Albania and unsuccessfully besieged the Castle of Kruje in an effort to defeat the resistance led by Skanderbeg. In the winter of 1450–1451, Murad II fell ill, and died in Edirne. He was succeeded by his son Mehmed II (1451–81).

Murad II

Władysław III (31 October 1424 – 10 November 1444), also known as Władysław of Varna was King of Poland from 1434, and King of Hungary and Croatia from 1440, until his death at the Battle of Varna. He was elected king over Ladislav "the Postumous" by the nobles, extending the reach of Jagiellonian influence from Lithuania through the Balkans. Even though the Ottoman's had agreed to a truce, he allowed himself to be talked into a preemptive strike against the Turks which was not fully planned out and moved against the enemy before his forces were prepared. He was killed on the battlefield; neither the king's body nor his armor was ever found.

Wladyslaw III

Jan Hunyadi

Jan Hunyadi (c. 1406 – 11 August 1456) was a leading Hungarian military and political figure in Central and Southeastern Europe during the 15th century. According to most contemporary sources, he was the son of a noble family of Romanian ancestry. He mastered his military skills on the southern borderlands of the Kingdom of Hungary that were exposed to Ottoman attacks. Appointed voivode of Transylvania and head of a number of southern counties, he assumed responsibility for the defense of the frontiers in 1441. Hunyadi adopted the Hussite method of using wagons for military purposes. He employed professional soldiers, but also mobilized local peasantry against invaders. These innovations contributed to his earliest successes against the Ottoman troops who were plundering the southern marches in the early 1440s. Although defeated in the battle of Varna in 1444 and in the second battle of Kosovo in 1448, his successful "Long Campaign" across the Balkan Mountains in 1443–44 and defense of Belgrade/Nándorfehérvár in 1456, against troops led personally by the Sultan established his reputation as a great general. The bells of Catholic and older Protestant churches are rung daily at noon to commemorate the Belgrade victory, although the pope had ordered this in advance, a week before the siege, in order to encourage the soldiers fighting for Christendom. When he resigned from this office in 1452, the sovereign awarded him with the first hereditary title (perpetual count of Beszterce) in the Kingdom of Hungary. He had by this time become one of the wealthiest landowners in the kingdom, and preserved his influence in the Diet up until his death.

Battle of Castillon

Date: 17 July 1453
Where: Castillon-la-Bataille, Gascony

Opponents:
Kingdom of England
   – approximately 6,000 – 10,000 men
Kingdom of France, Duchy of Brittany
   – approximately 7,000 men

Background:

The Battle of Castillon of 1453 was the last battle fought between the French and the English during the Hundred Years' War. This was the first battle in European history where cannons were a major factor in deciding the battle.

After the French capture of Bordeaux in 1451, the Hundred Years' War appeared to be at an end. However, after three hundred years of English rule the citizens of Bordeaux considered themselves English and sent messengers to Henry VI of England demanding he recapture the province.

On 17 October 1452, the Earl of Shrewsbury landed near Bordeaux with a force of 3,000 men-at-arms and archers. The French garrison was ejected by the citizens of Bordeaux, who then gleefully opened the gates to the English. Most of Gascony followed Bordeaux's example and welcomed the return of the English.

During the winter months Charles VII of France gathered his armies in preparation for the upcoming campaign season. When spring arrived Charles advanced toward Bordeaux simultaneously splitting his army into three separate forces marching along three different routes. Talbot, the Earl of Shrewsbury, received another 3,000 men in reinforcements to face this new problem, but it was still an inadequate number to hold back the thousands of French men on Gascony's borders. When the leading French army laid siege to Castillon, Talbot abandoned

English and French forces meet outside Castillon

his original plans (acceding to the pleas of the town commanders) and set out to relieve it. The French commander, Jean Bureau, fearing the arrival of Talbot ordered his 7,000 men to enclose their camp with a ditch and palisades; deploying his 300 cannon on the parapet. Despite an extraordinarily defensive setup by the French, and their large numerical superiority, they made no attempt to invade Castillon.

Talbot approached the French camp on 17 July 1453, arriving before his main body of troops with an advance guard of 1,300 mounted men. He routed a similar sized force of French francs-archers (militia) in the woods in front of the French encampment, giving his men a large morale boost.

Shrewsbury's troops had marched through the night and were resting in town when he received a report that the French army was in full retreat and hundreds of horsemen were fleeing the fortifications. From the town walls a huge dust cloud could be seen heading off into the distance. Unfortunately for him, they were only camp followers ordered to leave the camp before the upcoming battle.

Shrewsbury hastily reorganized his men and charged down towards the French camp, only to find the parapets defended by thousands of archers and crossbowmen, and hundreds of cannon. Surprised but undaunted, Shrewsbury gave the signal to attack the French army but was unable to participate because he was honoring his obligations of the conditions for being on parole.

English troops charged the camp, across a ditch, only to be met with a hail of arrows, quarrels, cannon and small arms fire. The concentrated fire could be explained by the fact that the ditch followed, probably by accident, the former bed of a small stream, giving a bastioned look to the defenses.

Once the battle started, Shrewsbury received some supporting troops from his advance infantry. After an hour the cavalry of the Breton army sent by the Duke of Brittany arrived and charged his right flank. The English gave way in a disorganized fashion, pursued by the main body of French troops.

During the rout Shrewsbury's horse was killed by a cannon ball and he fell trapped beneath it, until a Frenchman, a Francs Archer, recognized him and killed him with a hand-axe. His death, and the subsequent recapture of Bordeaux three months later, effectively brought the Hundred Years' War to a close.

Following Henry VI's episode of insanity in 1453, the subsequent outbreak of the War of

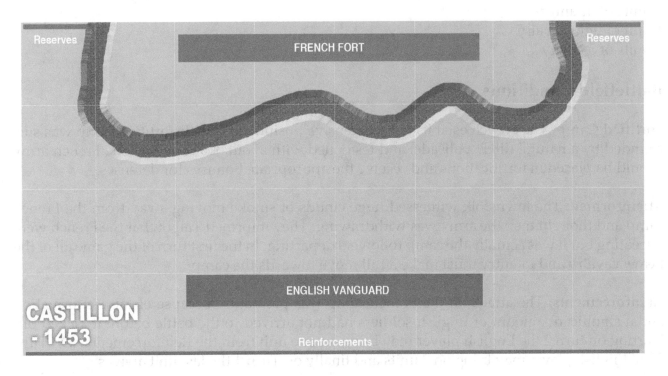

the Roses and the evident loss of the military ascendancy for the benefit of the French, the English were no longer in any position to pursue their claim to the French throne and lost all their land on the continent (except for Calais).

Wargaming the Battle of Castillon
Ratio- 1:1 (English:French)

English Order of Battle: 9 units

Commanding Officer:
John Talbot, Earl of Shrewsbury

Vanguard
2 units of heavy cavalry
2 units of infantry
1 unit of missile infantry

Reinforcements
2 units of infantry
2 units of missile infantry

French Order of Battle: 9 units

Commanding Officer:
Charles VII, Jean Bureau

Fort
4 units of missile infantry
2 units of infantry
1 unit of light cavalry
2 units of artillery

Reserve
2 units of heavy cavalry

Battlefield Conditions

Fortified Camp: The French established a defensive position and their fortified camp was surrounded by a natural ditch, palisade, and festooned with about 300 cannons. The French army should be placed in fortifications and receive the appropriate bonuses for defenses.

Misinformed: The townsfolk witnessed huge clouds of smoke moving away from the French camp and thought they the army was withdrawing. They informed Talbot that the French were retreating but it was actually the camp followers departing. In the first turn of the game all of the heavy cavalry and infantry must make a full move towards the camp.

Reinforcements: The attack on the French camp was premature because of false information and a significant amount of English soldiers had not arrived to the battle before it kicked off. Starting on turn 2 the English player may bring on one unit from the Reinforcements. On Turn 3 the English player may bring on 2 units and finally on Turn 4 the last unit arrives.

Reserve: The French had Breton cavalry allies who were sent by the Duke of Normandy to help relieve the attack on the camp. The Breton units are held in reserve and may arrive at the start of the turn by rolling a die. Beginning on turn 2 the French player will roll a die and on a 5+ the Breton cavalry arrives. On turn 3 the Bretons will arrive on a 4+, turn 4 a 3+, and so on always needing to roll a 2+ thereafter regardless of the turn number.

The Commanders

John Talbot, 1st Earl of Shrewsbury and *1st Earl of Waterford* (1384/1387 – 17 July 1453), known as "Old Talbot" was a noted English military commander during the Hundred Years' War, as well as the only Lancastrian Constable of France. He was appointed in 1445 by Henry VI (as king of France) as Constable of France. Taken hostage at Rouen in 1449 he promised never to wear armour against the French King again, and he was true to his word. However, though he did not personally fight, he continued to command English forces against the French. In England he was widely renowned as the best general King Henry VI had. The king relied upon his support at Dartford in 1452, and in 1450 to suppress Cade's Revolt. In 1452 he was ordered to Bordeaux to save the duchy of Aquitaine. He repaired castle garrisons facing mounting pressure from France, when some reinforcements arrived with his son John, Viscount Lisle in spring 1453. He was defeated and killed in July 1453 at the Battle of Castillon near Bordeaux, which effectively ended English rule in the duchy of Aquitaine, a principal cause of the Hundred Years' War. The victorious French generals raised a monument to Talbot on the field called Notre Dame de Talbot.

Jean Bureau (c. 1390 – 1463) was a French artillery commander active during the later years of the Hundred Years' War. Along with his brother, Gaspard, he is credited with making French artillery one of the most efficient in Europe. As Master Gunner of Artillery in the armies of Charles VII, Bureau acquired a reputation as an effective artillery officer during the Normandy campaign (1449–1450), when his bombardments helped capture the towns of Rouen, Harfleur, Honfleur, and aided in the French victory at Formigny. Bureau commanded the victorious French army at the decisive Battle of Castillon in 1453.

Jean Bureau

John Talbot

Battle of Towton

Date: 29 March 1461
Where: Towton, Yorkshire, England

War of the Roses

Opponents:

House of York – approximately 27,250 men
House of Lancaster – approximately 30,000 men

Background:

The War of the Roses was a conflict between the Houses of York and Lancaster vying for the English throne. Henry VI, the reigning king, was supported by the Lancastrians even though Henry was often indecisive and at times insane. Richard Plantagenet, 3rd Duke of York, felt that the country was going to ruin led by Henry and his attempts to remove the influential Lancastrians from powerful positions led directly to military conflict. Richard legitimized his claim to the throne after Henry's capture at the Battle of Northampton 1460 and the establishment of the Act of Accord; stating that in the event of Henry's death the Duke of York and his heirs would claim their rights to the English throne.

Richard's fate was to never see his rise to the throne as he and his second son Edmund, Earl of Rutland, were killed at the Battle of Wakefield. The command of the House of York passed to Richard's son Edward, Earl of March, who recently claimed a victory at the Battle of Mortimer's Cross. The Lancastrian army continued their march south freeing King Henry along their way to London but they were refused entry because of the reputation the soldiers earned looting towns and cities along their route. Edward's army was closing in on the Lancastrian force but they were short on provisions, so Henry and his allies returned to York to resupply. London opened its gates to Edward upon his arrival and several of the nobles viewed the Lancastrian behavior as an act of betrayal and legally accepted the Act of Accord making Edward a second king of England.

Lancastrian forces

Edward needed to physically remove Henry from the throne and his first step was to offer any Lancastrian commoners amnesty if they renounced Henry as the king. He then ordered his followers to assemble an army and marched to York to take back his family's city and depose Henry. The Yorkist army took three routes to York with Lord Fauconberg moving first in an attempt to clear a way for the main force led by Edward. The second force was under John de Mowbray, 3rd Duke of Norfolk, who was sent to raise additional troops before meeting Edward. The third

Yorkist forces on the move

group led by Warwick marched west of the main body through the Midlands recruiting soldiers as they moved.

Lead elements of the main body moved up to the Aire River and the Ferry bridge spanning the river needed to be rebuilt in order for it to be used by the army. A small Lancastrian force of about 500 men lead by John Clifford, 9th Baron de Clifford, attacked the Yorkists and forced them to retire back towards the main body. Edward returned with a larger force but the superior numbers were irrelevant because of the narrow frontage of the bridge that they fought over. Edward ordered Fauconberg to take some horsemen and cross the river at Castleford in order to flank the Lancastrians defending the bridge. The Yorkists surrounded their enemy and Clifford was forced to retreat only to be rundown and killed at Dinting Dale. Now that the Yorkists were free from attack they were able to repair the bridge and continue their journey towards York. Edward and his army arrived at Sherburn-in-Elmet and spent the night camped in the area while the Lancastrian army marched to Tadcaster approximately 2 miles north of Towton and rested for the night.

The Lancastrian army was led by Henry Beaufort, 3rd Duke of Somerset while King Henry remained in York awaiting the outcome of the battle. Both forces deployed on a plateau between the villages of Saxton and Towton with plenty of open fields and small roads for both forces to maneuver. The Lancastrian army deployed on the north side of the Towton Dale; this allowed the army to easily defend the London-Towton and the old Roman roads leading towards the city of York. In front of them lay a valley that they used as a protective ditch with their flanks tied in by marshes and the additional protection of steep banks of the Cock Beck on their right

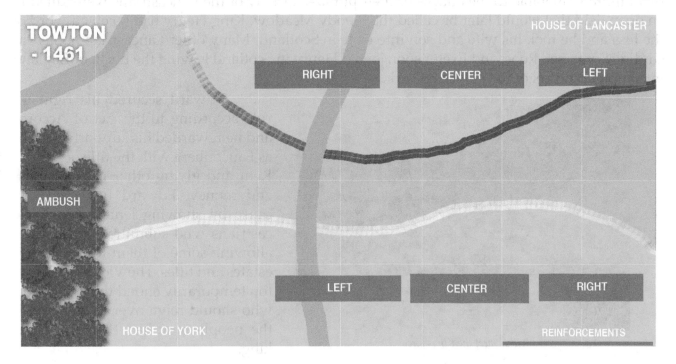

side. The Lancastrian position did not allow them to see beyond the southern ridge of the dale and their narrow frontage deprived them of the numerical superiority. The Yorkists appeared as the Lancastrians finished their deployment and the southern ridge was full of formed-up ranks just as it began to snow.

Fauconberg ordered his archers to step forward and open up the battle with an intense volley of arrows. With the wind in their favor the arrows hit the mass of Lancastrian troops stationed on the hill but their return fire was ineffective because of the range combined with the wind and snow in their faces. The Lancastrian archers were unable to witness the effect of their volleys so they continued to fire until they depleted their arrows. The Yorkist archers would reuse the enemy's arrows laying in front of them and continue to pepper the Lancastrians with their deadly fire.

The Lancastrians realized they were losing the archery duel and decided to advance into melee with the Yorkists. The Yorkist archers fired one last volley at the advancing enemy and returned to the safety of their lines behind the men-at-arms leaving thousands of arrows in the ground as obstructions for the attacking Lancastrians. The Yorkists prepared themselves to receive the charge when their left flank was hit by Lancastrian cavalry ambushing them from the Castle Hill Wood. The left flank began to crumble when Edward repositioned himself and took command saving the situation from the brink of disaster.

The hand-to-hand combat was brutal and the numerically superior Lancastrians continued to throw fresh troops into the fray eventually forcing the Yorkists to retreat back up the southern ridge. The battle raged indecisively for three hours when Norfolk arrived marching up the Old London Road with fresh Yorkist soldiers. The Lancastrians did not see the reinforcements until it was too late and the Yorkist troops crashed into their left flank. The Lancastrians continued to defy the Yorkist army but eventually the line broke and the survivors fled the battlefield.

The fleeing Lancastrians removed pieces of their armor to run faster but this only made them more vulnerable to the attacks of their pursuers. Many of the Lancastrians were killed in an open field that would later be called the Bloody Meadow. King Henry had received word of the loss and he took his wife and son into exile in Scotland. Many other Lancastrian nobles including Somerset, Roos, and Exeter soon joined Henry in Scotland leaving the north of England in complete control of the House of York.

Rebels meet the Kings forces

Edward secured his right to rule according to the Act of Accord and he rewarded his supporters such as Fauconberg with the title of Earl of Kent and giving other gentry lands and money. Edward furthered his cause by showing leniency to Lancastrians who submitted to his rule allowing some of them to keep their estates and titles. The Victory at Towton temporarily ended the dispute of who should reign over England and the people now had their one true king.

Wargaming the Battle of Towton
Ratio- 1:1 (Yorkists:Lancastrians)

House of York Order of Battle: 12 units

Commanding Officer:
Edward IV of England (Right Flank), Earl of Warwick (Center), Lord Fauconberg (Left Flank)
John de Mowbray, 3rd Duke of Norfolk (Reinforcements)

Right Flank
2 units of missile infantry
1 unit of infantry

Left Flank
2 units of missile infantry
1 unit of infantry

Center
2 units of missile infantry
1 unit of infantry

Reinforcements
2 units of infantry
1 unit of heavy cavalry

Yorkist Infantry

House of Lancaster Order of Battle: 12 units

Commanding Officer:
Henry Beaufort, 3rd Duke of Somerset (Center), Earl of Northumberland (Right Flank)
Duke of Exeter (Left Flank)

Right Flank
2 units of missile infantry
1 unit of infantry

Left Flank
2 units of missile infantry
1 unit of infantry

Center
2 units of missile infantry
2 units of infantry

Ambush
2 units of heavy cavalry

Battlefield Conditions

Ambush: Lancastrian cavalry were hiding in the Castle Hill Woods waiting for the opportune time to spring their trap. At the start of any turn the Lancastrian player may deploy both units of cavalry in the Castle Hill Woods. If any Yorkist unit moves towards or into the woods the unit should be stopped and the Lancastrian cavalry units should be placed just outside of charge range revealing the ambush.

Favorable Winds: The Yorkist archers had the advantage of head winds and because of this they should have an increased range.

Limited ammunition: TheLancastrian archers fired all of their arrows during the battle forcing the army to advance into melee. The army could be given a limited amount of ammunition for the game forcing them to use their arrows wisely.

Reinforcements: Norfolk was moving around the country recruiting fresh troops and arrived to the battle late but just in time to save the Yorkist cause. His units are held in reserve and may arrive at the start of the turn by rolling a die. Beginning on turn 2 the Yorkist player will roll a die and on a 5+ Norfolk arrives. On turn 3 Norfolk will arrive on a 4+, turn 4 a 3+, and soon always needing to roll a 2+ thereafter regardless of the turn number.

Infantry ready to strike

The Commanders

Edward IV (28 April 1442 – 9 April 1483) was the King of England from 4 March 1461 until 3 October 1470, and again from 11 April 1471 until his death in 1483. He was the first Yorkist King of England. The first half of his rule was marred by the violence associated with the Wars of the Roses, but he overcame the Lancastrian challenge to the throne at Tewkesbury in 1471 to reign in peace until his sudden death in 1483. Before becoming king, he was 4th Duke of York, 7th Earl of March, 5th Earl of Cambridge and 9th Earl of Ulster. He was also the 65th Knight of the Order of the Golden Fleece. Edward did not face any further rebellions after his restoration, as the Lancastrian line had virtually been extinguished, and the only rival left was Henry Tudor, who was living in exile. He fell fatally ill at Easter 1483, but lingered on long enough to add some codicils to his will, the most important being his naming of his brother Richard, Duke of Gloucester, as Protector after his death. He died on 9 April 1483 and was buried in St George's Chapel, Windsor Castle. He was succeeded by his twelve-year-old son, Edward V of England (who was never crowned) and then by his brother, Richard.

Henry Beaufort, 3rd Duke of Somerset (26 January 1436 – 15 May 1464) was an important Lancastrian military commander during the English War of the Roses. He is sometimes numbered the 2nd Duke of Somerset, since the title was re-created for his father after his uncle died. He also held the subsidiary titles of 5th Earl of Somerset, 2nd Marquis of Dorset and 2nd Earl of Dorset. During his absence the Yorkists had won the battle of Northampton, but Somerset joined the Lancastrians at Pontefract in December 1460, captured a portion of the Yorkist forces at Worksop on the 21 December, and won the Lancastrian victory at the Battle of Wakefield on 30 December. He marched south with Margaret and fought at the second Battle of St Albans (17 February 1461). This second victory was not followed up, the Lancastrians retired north, and on 29 March Edward IV won the battle of Towton (29 March 1461).

King Edward IV

Arms of Henry Beaufort

Battle of Tewkesbury

Date: 4 May 1471
Where: Tewkesbury, Gloucestershire, England

Opponents:
House of York – approximately 5,000 men
House of Lancaster – approximately 6,000 men

Background:

The War of the Roses was a conflict between the two rival houses of Lancaster and York fighting for power and ultimately for the English throne since the 1450s. In 1461, Edward, Earl of March, was declared King Edward IV and defeated the House of Lancaster at the Battle of Towton. This was not the end of the Lancastrian threat since it took Edward IV until 1464 to temporarily secure his throne when Henry VI was captured and imprisoned. Henry's queen, Margaret of Anjou, was then exiled to France making Edward IV feel secure in his victory. Unfortunately, Edward's marriage to Elizabeth Woodville and the elevation of his new queen's family into powerful positions enraged Edward's cousin the Earl of Warwick and he decided to support Edward's brother, George, Duke of Clarence, in a coup. Edward was imprisoned briefly but Warwick quickly realized that Clarence was unfit for duty so Edward was released and he resumed his rule as king. Edward IV briefly reconciled with Warwick and Clarence but soon accused them of treachery and forced them to flee to France.

Edward IV's troops prepare to finish the job

Warwick realized his only way of regaining his power in England was to ally himself with Margaret of Anjou. The sworn enemies forgave each other because of their common interests and Louis XI of France offered his support to the Lancastrian cause with men and money. After an oath of allegiance to Henry VI was sworn on a fragment of the True Cross in Angers Cathedral, Warwick assembled an army landing it in West Country on 13 September 1470. King Edward IV marched south to confront Warwick when he received word that Warwick's brother John, Marquess of Montagu, had defected along with his large army forcing Edward to flee England for Flanders.

Warwick released King Henry and installed him back on the throne at Westminster palace. In November 1470, Parliament declared that Henry's descendants were heirs to the throne leaving Clarence with no chance to become king. Unbeknownst to Warwick, Clarence had secretly been forgiven by his brother King Edward IV, setting up a new alliance that will prove deadly for Warwick.

Charles of Burgundy supported Edward's cause and gave him money, ships, and men to aid him in his struggles to retake his

Yorkist infantry moves forward

throne. With 36 ships and 1,200 men he landed near York on 14 March and began his long march south gathering troops along the way. Edward successfully evaded Montagu's army and outpaced Warwick's force entering London unopposed placing Henry back in the Tower of London. With London secure Edward turned to face Warwick and his brother and at the Battle of Barnet. The thick fog caused massive confusion which led to Montagu's death in the battle and Warwick's demise as he attempted to remount his horse during an escape.

On 14 April, the same day as the Battle of Barnet, Queen Margaret and her son Prince Edward landed in England and they moved north in the hope of joining forces in Wales with the Lancastrians led by Jasper Tudor. Two days after Margaret's landing, Edward received word of the invasion force and even though several troops were on leave after the Battle of Barnet he was able to assemble enough troops at Windsor to push forward. The Lancastrian army moved towards Wales wishing to cross the Severn River at Gloucester, but anticipating this movement Edward IV sent word to the Governor, Sir Richard Beauchamp, to close the gates and refuse entry to Margaret and her supporters. On 3 May the Lancastrians reached Gloucester and were

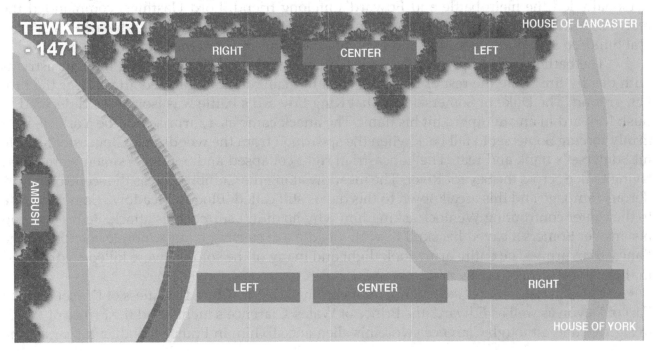

denied entry causing them to force-march 10 miles to Tewkesbury about halfway to the bridge at Upton-upon-Severn.

The King's Standard and troops

The long marches and the hot days exhausted both armies so when the Lancastrians reached Tewkesbury they camped for the evening. Most of King Edward's men were mounted and elected to fight on foot making them more fit for battle than their enemy. The Yorkists pushed hard into the evening to arrive just three miles from the Lancastrians and Margaret knew that they could flee no further without exposing their rear to attack.

On the morning of 4 May, the Lancastrians deployed in a defensive formation approximately a mile south of Tewkesbury with the Avon and Severn Rivers laying in their rear. Tewkesbury Abbey was just behind the Lancastrian center and the Gobes Hall farmhouse marked the center of the army. The front of the Lancastrian army was broken up by hedges, woods, and embankments providing extra strength for the position of the force. The Lancastrian army was approximately 6,000 men and divided into three 'battles' with the right battle commanded by the Duke of Somerset, the center led by Baron Wenlock and Prince Edward, and the left battle commanded by the Earl of Devon. The Colnbrook stream flowed through Somerset's position making some of the ground difficult to navigate while Devon's battle occupied a low ridge with the small Swilgate River protecting his open flank.

The Yorkists had about 5,000 men and similar to the Lancastrians they organized themselves into three battles. The vanguard of the army was led by Richard, Duke of Gloucester, Edward's youngest brother, who successfully led a battle at Barnet. Edward along with Clarence personally led the main battle and Edward's lifelong friend, Lord Hastings, commanded the rear. The Yorkist left flank had thick woods and worried about an ambush Edward IV sent several hundred spearmen to occupy and deny his enemy from using them.

The battle opened up with the Yorkist archers and artillery showering the Lancastrians with deadly fire while the rest of the army tried to maintain an organized attack over the broken ground. The Duke of Somerset saw that King Edward's battle was isolated and decided to push forward in an attempt to hit his flank. The attack came as a surprise but the Yorkists held firmly forcing Somerset to fall back when the spearmen from the woods and Gloucester's battle hit Somerset's flank and rear. The Lancastrian right collapsed and Somerset's men were killed trying to flee across the Severn River. The meadow along the Colnbrook was the scene of a murderous rampage and this area known to this day is still called 'Bloody Meadow'. Somerset rode to the center confronting Wenlock asking him why he didn't support his attack. Before hearing his answer Somerset caved his skull in with a battle axe causing a huge morale collapse in the Lancastrian army. The entire army took flight and many of the soldiers were killed or drowned in the waters during their escape.

The Lancastrians lost several nobles including John Beaufort, Marquess of Dorset and the Earl of Devon as well as Edward, the Prince of Wales. Clarence's men found the Prince of Wales in a grove and although Clarence swore his allegiance to him in France less than a year ago he had no compunction about executing him. Other Lancastrians such as Hugh Courtenay and Sir John Langstrother were found after the battle seeking sanctuary in Tewkesbury Abbey and were put to death after perfunctory trials.

Edward IV's job to repulse the Lancastrians was not complete and he needed to beat Jasper Tudor and Thomas Neville (the Bastard of Fauconberg) before securing his throne. On 21 May as Edward passed through London, Henry VI had died the night before in the Tower of London possibly by the hands of or by the order of Richard of Gloucester. The Lancastrian royal bloodline had almost been eradicated from history but Margaret Beaufort's son Henry Tudor remained in exile in Brittany until Edward's death and eventually became the King of England.

A clash of cavalry on the flank

Wargaming the Battle of Tewkesbury
Ratio- 1:1 (Yorkists:Lancastrians)

House of York Order of Battle: 9 units

Commanding Officers:
Edward IV of England (Center); Richard, Duke of Gloucester (Left Flank); Lord Hastings (Right Flank)

Right Flank	Left Flank	Center
1 unit of heavy cavalry	1 unit of heavy cavalry	1 unit of heavy cavalry
1 unit of missile infantry	1 unit of missile infantry	1 unit of missile infantry
1 unit of infantry	1 unit of infantry	1 unit of artillery

Ambush
1 unit of infantry

House of Lancaster Order of Battle: 9 units

Commanding Officers:
Edmund Beaufort, 4th Duke of Somerset (Right Flank), Baron Wenlock (Center), Earl of Devon (Left Flank)

Right Flank	Left Flank	Center
1 unit of heavy cavalry	1 unit of heavy cavalry	1 unit of heavy cavalry
1 unit of missile infantry	1 unit of missile infantry	1 unit of missile infantry
1 unit of infantry	1 unit of infantry	2 units of infantry

Battlefield Conditions

Ambush: Edward sent 200 spearmen into the nearby woods to prevent the Lancastrians from springing any surprises. During a pivotal moment in the battle they ended up leaping from the woods and surprising the Lancastrians. The Yorkist player may hold one unit of infantry from the center force in ambush and deploy them in the woods at the start of any turn. If any Lancastrian unit moves towards or into the woods the unit should be stopped and the Yorkist infantry unit should be placed just outside of charge range revealing the ambush.

The Commanders

Edward IV (28 April 1442 – 9 April 1483) Edward was one of the few male members of his dynasty to die of natural causes. Both Edward's father and brother were killed at the Battle of Wakefield, while his grandfather and another brother were executed for treason. Edward's two sons were imprisoned and disappeared (presumed killed) within a year of Edward's death. The king's youngest brother, Richard, (later Richard III) was famously killed in battle against Henry Tudor at Bosworth Field. Soon after Henry Tudor took the throne as Henry VII, he married Edward's eldest daughter Elizabeth of York, who was at that point the family heiress. Through her, the Plantagenet family and the House of York continue in the line of English and British sovereigns.

Edward IV had ten children by Elizabeth Woodville, seven of whom survived him. They were declared illegitimate by Parliament in 1483, clearing the way for Richard III to become King. The Act, Titulus Regius (King's Title), was quickly repealed by Henry VII, thereby legitimising those whom that Act had made illegitimate. In fact, Henry Tudor not only had the Act repealed without being read, he made it a crime to possess a copy or even to mention it.

Henry Beaufort, 3rd Duke of Somerset Somerset had a son, Charles, with a mistress named Joan Hill. Charles, who was given the family name of Somerset, was later created Earl of Worcester in 1514. From him descend the Earls and Marquesses of Worcester and later the Dukes of Beaufort, who are currently the last male-line descendants of the Plantagenet and the Second House of the Counts of Anjou. In 1485, some twenty-one years after his death, Somerset, along with Jasper Tudor, had all acts of attainder against him annulled in the first Parliament of Henry VII.

Battle of Bosworth Field

Date: 22 August 1485
Where: Ambion Hill, Market Bosworth, England

Opponents:

House of York – approximately 10,000 men
House of Lancaster – approximately 5,000 men
Stanley Family – approximately 6,000 men

Background:

The Battle of Bosworth Field was the last major battle during the War of the Roses which consisted of the House of Lancaster and the House of York. Throughout the 15th Century the ideology of selfless service to the King of England eroded as families vied for power and presented their own 'legitimate' heirs to the throne. The feudal system of raising armies required that all able-bodied men would report to their lord's call to arms so the subjects' loyalties were based on the interests of their own lord. A king would only be able to keep his throne through manipulating the aristocracy with gifts and clever diplomacy.

The Houses of York and Lancaster waged a bloody war for control of England for the better part of thirty years and in aftermath of the Battle of Tewkesbury in 1471, King Henry VI and his son Edward of Lancaster died leaving the Yorkist king, Edward IV, in complete control of the nation. Edward ruled with an iron fist and alienated the Tudor family and Lancastrian nobles by branding Jasper and his nephew Henry traitors, forcing them to flee the country. Jasper and Henry sailed for France but strong winds landed them in Brittany where a sympathetic Duke Francis II remanded them in custody with the hopes of using them as a bargaining tool for England's aid against Brittany's conflict with France.

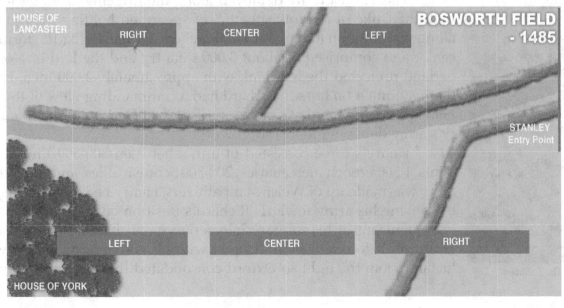

The King's forces approach

Twelve years later King Edward IV died on 9 April 1483 and his oldest son, Edward V, at twelve years old became the new King. A Royal Council was established to steward the throne until Edward V came of age. The Woodville family, relatives of Edward IV's widow Elizabeth, began to plot against the young king in an attempt to gain control of the council. Edward V's uncle, Richard, Duke of Gloucester stepped in the role of Protector but he had his own plans for securing his future. Two of the Woodvilles along with members of the council were executed for treason and Richard consolidated his power by convincing Parliament that the marriage between Edward IV and Elizabeth was illegitimate. This act disqualified Edward V from being king and on 26 June 1483 King Richard III was proclaimed King of England.

Nobles' loyal to Edward IV perceived Richard III as a usurper and over the next two years plotted uprisings with the hopes of unseating this unpopular king. Henry Tudor, residing in Brittany, was an active participant in the rebellion but his proposed landing on 10 October was cancelled because of bad weather. It was not until the death of Richard's queen, Anne Neville, and Richard's plan to marry his niece, Elizabeth, that Henry was forced to spring into action and sail across the channel with almost 2,000 men in the hope of stopping the marriage and placing the English crown on his own head.

Henry's landing in Wales went without incident and along his march towards the English border he increased the ranks of his army with loyal supporters and dissenters. Along the route Henry had been secretly meeting and communicating with the Stanley Family to gain and organize their support. Meanwhile, Richard became fully aware of Henry's arrival and sent out messengers to inform his lords to prepare for the impending battle. The Royal Army marched to meet Henry's forces and camped on Ambion Hill which Henry thought was a tactically advantageous position.

The Standards

The Yorkist army deployed along the ridgeline from west to east with the Duke of Norfolk's' battle' of spearmen holding the right flank along with cannon and about 1,200 archers. Richard's 'battle' formed the center and comprised of about 3,000 infantry and the Earl of Northumberland protected the left flank with approximately 4,000 men, many of them mounted on horses. Richard had a commanding view of the battlefield witnessing Stanley's army on display at Dadlington Hill and Henry's army deploying to his southwest.

Henry's force consisted of a mix between 300-500 English dissidents, 1,800 French mercenaries, 200-300 Scottish allies, and the rest of the army was made up of Welsh sympathizers. Henry began the engagement by moving his army towards Richard's position on Ambion Hill. Henry was cognizant of his military inexperience and handed command over to Oxford before retiring to the rear with his bodyguard. Stanley was reluctan to join the fight so Oxford consolidated the army and moved his infantry to attack the center with his cavalry protecting the flanks.

Richard used his cannons to wreak havoc on Oxford's advance around the marsh and Norfolk committed his troops to the fight with Richard's battle in support. The two armies clashed under a torrent of archery and Oxford's men began to push Norfolk back. Richard called upon Northumberland to support the attack but either due to personal reasons or the terrain hindering his advance his forces did not move. Henry took this opportunity to ride towards Stanley with the hopes of bringing his forces into the conflict. Richard elected that killing Henry would end this battle and save his crown so he took approximately 800-1,000 knights and led a headlong charge crashing into Henry's bodyguards. Stanley recognized the opportunity watching Richard separate from his army so he decided to press the advantage and surround the king. The gambit proved successful as Richard was hacked down and news of his death quickly spread disintegrating his forces.

Henry was crowned king on the battlefield after the engagement and proceeded to establish his rule as the new monarch. He went on to marry Elizabeth and restoring her title as princess aligning the two houses and beginning the long reign of the Tudor dynasty.

The clash of the infantry

Wargaming the Battle of Bosworth Field
Ratio- 1:1 (Yorkists:Lancastrians/Stanley's)

House of York Order of Battle: 9 units

Commanding Officers:
Richard III of England (Center), John Howard, 1st Duke of Norfolk (Right Flank), Henry Percy, 4th Earl of Northumberland (Left Flank)

Right Flank	**Left Flank**	**Center**
2 units of infantry	2 units of heavy cavalry	2 units of infantry
Unit of missile infantry	1 unit of light cavalry	1 unit of missile infantry
1 unit of artillery		

House of Lancaster Order of Battle: 4 units

Commanding Officers:
Henry Tudor, Earl of Richmond and John Savage (Left Flank), John de Vere, 13th Earl of Oxford (Center), Gilbert Talbot (Right Flank)

Right Flank	**Left Flank**	**Center**
1 unit of heavy cavalry	1 unit of heavy cavalry	1 unit of missile infantry
		1 unit of infantry

Stanley Family Order of Battle: 5 units

Commanding Officers:
Thomas Stanley, 2nd Baron Stanley (Rear), Sir William Stanley (Vanguard)

Vanguard	**Rear**
2 units of heavy cavalry	1 unit of infantry
1 unit of infantry	1 unit of missile infantry

Battlefield Conditions

Stanley's Force: The Stanley's were indecisive when or if they should attack. Their forces are held off table and when the first Lancastrian unit is destroyed they will enter play the following turn on the side of the Lancastrians in the Yorkists right flank.

The Commanders

Richard III (2 October 1452 – 22 August 1485) was King of England from 1483 until his death in 1485, at the age of 32, at the Battle of Bosworth Field. He was the last king of the House of York and the last of the Plantagenet dynasty. His defeat at Bosworth Field, the last decisive battle of the War of the Roses, marked the end of the Middle Ages in England.

When his brother King Edward IV died in April 1483, Richard was named Lord Protector of the realm for Edward's son and successor, the 12-year-old Edward V. As the young king travelled to London from Ludlow, Richard met and escorted him to lodgings in the Tower of London, where Edward V's was joined by his brother Richard of Shrewsbury. In the midst of making arrangement for Edward's coronation, Richard maneuvered to have Edward IV's marriage to Elizabeth Woodville declared invalid, making their children illegitimate and ineligible for the throne. On 25 June, an assembly of Lords and commoners endorsed the claims. Richard III was crowned on 6 July 1483, while the young princes were not seen in public after August, and accusations circulated that the boys had been murdered on Richard's orders, giving rise to the legend of the Princes in the Tower.

Of the two major rebellions against Richard, the first, in October 1483, was led by allies of Edward IV and Richard's former ally, Henry Stafford, 2nd Duke of Buckingham; but the revolt quickly collapsed. In August 1485, Henry Tudor and his uncle, Jasper Tudor, led a second rebellion against Richard. Henry Tudor landed in southern Wales with a small contingent of French troops and marched through his birthplace, Pembrokeshire, recruiting soldiers. Henry's force engaged Richard's army and defeated it at the Battle of Bosworth Field in Leicestershire. Richard was struck down in the conflict, making him the last English king to die in battle on home soil and the first since Harold II was killed at the Battle of Hastings in 1066. After the battle Richard's corpse was taken to Leicester and buried without pomp. His original tomb is believed to have been destroyed during the Reformation, and his remains were lost for more than five centuries.

In 2012, an archaeological excavation was conducted on a city council car park on the site once occupied by Greyfriars Priory Church. The University of Leicester identified the skeleton found in the excavation as that of Richard III and his remains were reburied in Leicester Cathedral on 26 March 2015.

Richard III

Henry VII (28 January 1457 – 21 April 1509) was King of England, ruled the Principality of Wales (until 29 November 1489) and Lord of Ireland from his seizing the crown on 22 August 1485 until his death on 21 April 1509, as the first monarch of the House of Tudor. Henry won the throne when his forces defeated the forces of Richard III at the Battle of Bosworth Field, the culmination of the War of the Roses. Henry was the last king of England to win his throne on the field of battle. He cemented his claim by marrying Elizabeth of York, daughter of Edward IV and niece of Richard III. Henry was successful in restoring the power and stability of the English monarchy after the political upheavals of the civil wars known as the Wars of the Roses. He founded the Tudor dynasty and, after a reign of nearly 24 years, was peacefully succeeded by his son, Henry VIII.

Henry VII

Look for more books from Winged Hussar Publishing, LLC – E-books, paperbacks and Limited Edition hardcovers. The best in history, science fiction and fantasy at:

https://wingedhussarpublishing.com

or follow us on Facebook at:

Winged Hussar Publishing LLC

Or on twitter at:

WingHusPubLLC

For information and upcoming publications

The author and publishers would like to thank the following people and companies for their support in this book through photos or permissions:

Bill Davis
Fabio Sprezia
Fireforge Games
Giuseppe Rava
Ian Gray
Kevin Krause
Malcolm Gray
Matthew Sullivan
Scott Perry
Testudo Miniatures
Warlord Games